Vegan 101

HEATHER BELL $ JENNY ENGEL
of Spork Foods

Vegan 101

A Vegan Cookbook

Photography by Kate Lewis

FALL RIVER PRESS

New York

FALL RIVER PRESS

New York

An Imprint of Sterling Publishing Co., Inc.
1166 Avenue of the Americas
New York, NY 10036

FALL RIVER PRESS and the distinctive Fall River Press logo
are registered trademarks of Barnes & Noble Booksellers, Inc.

ISBN 978-1-4351-6815-2

For information about custom editions, special sales, and premium and
corporate purchases, please contact Sterling Special Sales at 800-805-5489
or specialsales@sterlingpublishing.com.

Manufactured in China

2 4 6 8 10 9 7 5 3 1

sterlingpublishing.com

Food photography by Kate Lewis and group photo on page 215 by Jiro Schneider.
Back cover author photo by Jeremie Brilliant.

Portrait photography © Diana Ragland, p.18; Susan Weingartner, p.19;
Melissa Schwartz, p.20; Robyn Von Swank, p.25; Follow Your Heart, p.26.

To Jer & Joshie,

for making our hearts happy everyday

Contents

Roll Call!

Jenny and Heather are the *Car Talk* of vegan cooking. You spend the entire class laughing, and on the way out are amazed to realize how much you've learned. ASHER B., CEO, pollution.tv

I love Spork Foods, from their vibrant, positive personalities, to the high quality of their delicious recipes! I enjoy the variety of cuisines with their recipes, from Indian, Thai, French, Italian, and more! KIM K., Director of Public Relations, Four Seasons Hotel Los Angeles at Beverly Hills

Heather and Jenny are creative geniuses in the kitchen. Every one of their recipes that I have made has been easily executed and left my non-vegan diners wanting more. They are educators, entertainers, and chefs who make you feel like part of their family. JENN K., Regional Director, LEGO Brand Retail

Our entire Anthem staff looks forward to the cooking class put on by Jenny & Heather. Year after year their work is educational and super entertaining. SARAH J., SBO, CA Wellness Lead, NIFS

Every Spork Foods class is like getting a personal cooking lesson from friends, and always guaranteed to include delicious food, fun facts, and good times. STEPHANIE D., Vegan Lifestyle Expert & Author

Heather and Jenny make every class so accessible, fun, and delicious that I forget that I was once totally intimidated by the concept of vegan cooking. JIM H., Human Resources Director

My husband and I love taking Spork Foods classes because we always learn something new and enjoy dining on the delicious eats in their lovely West Hollywood studio. JENNIFER C., Food Editor, *VegNews* Magazine

I always learn tons from the Spork Foods classes about food history, its origins, and how food chemistry works—I learn how to cook, technique, from the best knives and pots to how to get that garlic smell off your hands. That sounds boring and educational, but the sisters are so funny, it's always a blast and helps the knowledge really sink in. CAROLINE S., Executive Recruiter

The classes are peppered with intelligent facts and fun, useful techniques to make your journey into plant-based food as seamless as possible. I've been telling my patients that cooking with Spork exceeded my expectations about learning how to combine common ingredients to create unexpected and highly fulfilling meals. AYDIN B., Acupuncturist

I love spending weekend afternoons cooking with Jenny and Heather because I get an education, a delicious cruelty-free meal, a comedy sketch, and two temporary sisters all in a few short hours! SCOTTIE W., Fitness Industry Corporate Strategist

Jenny and Heather's classes are the tipping point to you accidentally converting your whole family to plant-based food. COLE M., Author & Illustrator

Introduction

Welcome, class! We want to motivate you to start cooking and enjoying the process of creating quick and nourishing meals from scratch. If you're like us, dinnertime prep begins around noon when you start thinking about what you'll be hungry for later. This book is full of easy recipes that you can make any night of the week.

We opened our sister-owned vegan cooking school, Spork Foods, in 2007 not really knowing who would walk in the door. About a decade later here we are, teaching both vegans and omnivores from all walks of life, and with all skill levels, how to cook.

The personal connection we make with our students is what drives and inspires us to keep doing what we do. (We've included a handful of really fun Take It From Us profiles of some of our amazing students in Chapter 1!) We teach about 10,000 people a year both in our kitchen in West Hollywood and at universities, health care companies, hotels, corporations, markets, and restaurants worldwide. We see that there is a huge demand for healthy food that has all of the flavor, color, and texture we can't live without. Our recipes are designed to be approachable and familiar to all palates.

Throughout the years many students have come through our doors. Our students range from longtime vegans to new cooks who just want to eat healthier, people who can't cook and were urged to attend by their spouses, and others looking for more exciting recipes to work into their everyday lives. The truth is that we all know eating a wide variety of plant-based foods is good for you, but it's also great for the planet, kinder to animals, and beneficial to your health. By the end of a cooking class with us, all these strangers who have now become friends are sitting together, enjoying a meal with a new perspective on vegan cuisine, and leaving full and satisfied.

Because teaching cooking classes is what we do, the recipes in this book are geared toward anyone who is looking to explore the world of vegan cooking.

Before beginning, preparation is key. Here are some tips for success that we've heard work wonders for our cooking students:

1. If you're new to cooking in general, start with one recipe at a time, instead of attacking a whole meal. It will ensure you're not overwhelmed in the kitchen.

2. Read the recipe the whole way through before diving in. If you're planning on using puff pastry that needs thawing time, or making a dish that needs chilling time, you want to ensure you won't have any surprises and have to wait.

3. Stock your pantry and refrigerator with a wide variety of spices, vinegars, oils, and other staples. It makes cooking easier in general because then you're not driving to the grocery store for every little ingredient.

4. Get a good chef's knife! It's your most basic and trusty tool in the kitchen and will help meal prep go smoothly.

5. If you're overwhelmed easily in the kitchen, invest in some prep bowls of different sizes where you can measure out ingredients and organize yourself even before turning on the oven.

We often train chefs at large corporations or hotels who are looking to incorporate some vegan options on their menus. Sometimes the request is driven by customer or staff demand, and other times it's because a high-level executive had a life-changing experience and now wants to share that knowledge with others. When we arrive to train chefs, we show up in our pink chef coats, all smiles. Some chefs scowl at having to learn about a new way of eating, and others embrace it. In every single instance chefs have come to us on the side and confessed that they actually eat mostly veg at home and really enjoy it. We go into each scenario sensitive to the fact that not everyone is comfortable with preparing an unfamiliar cuisine, but throughout the experience the food speaks for itself. When we hear that the recipes are tasty, and not just for vegan food, then we've done our job. We don't preach or force people to change their lifestyle, but we know that the more positive eating experiences people have with vegan meals, the more open they are to giving them another shot in the future.

One of our most memorable cooking class experiences was with an amazing non-vegan gal who had just moved to Los Angeles and "couldn't cook to save her life." She was a workaholic and decided that a cooking class would be a great way to see what Los Angeles was all about and possibly make new friends in the process. She didn't choose to attend our class because it was vegan, she had just heard about it being a fun and comfortable atmosphere. Fast-forward seven years, and she's taken dozens of our classes and is now a confident cook who throws dinner parties regularly and has even invited us over to taste her cooking.

We hope you have many memorable meals and dirty pages by the time you cook your way through our book!

XO,
Heather & Jenny

1

School Is In Session!

POP QUIZ! Name one good reason to eat vegan meals. Surprise! It doesn't matter what your reason is because *all* answers are correct. If you responded: "Plant foods make me feel nourished, sated, and energized," then you aced this one. Maybe you answered: "For the animals." Guess what? You get an A-plus, too. Even "Plants just taste good" deserves high marks. Whatever your reasons for integrating more edible bounty from the plant kingdom into your diet, they're the right ones.

Do you already relish the simple pleasures of grains, beans, fruits, bread, pasta, rice, and vegetables? Nice work! These familiar favorites, bursting with nutritional value and wholesome flavors, form the foundation of stellar vegan eats. To keep mealtimes interesting, this book guides you through thrilling terrain with easy recipes to add even more color (more nutrients!) and complexity (new delicious flavors for your palate to enjoy!) to the everyday dishes you currently make.

This first chapter is designed to introduce you to terms and ingredients you may not already be familiar with. Once you're armed with your handy vegan vernacular, you'll feel confident to dive in and get busy in the kitchen whenever inspiration strikes.

Ready to get schooled in creative cooking? Class commences!

MEAT(S) OF THE MATTER

Meatiness isn't a quality reserved exclusively for animal products; vegetables, too, have the ability to take on meaty characteristics with just a splash of seasoning and a turn in the sauté pan. Vegan proteins made from beans and grains offer yet more culinary versatility—especially tofu, seitan, and tempeh. Get acquainted with this tasty triumvirate and explore whole new worlds of texture and flavor.

Tofu

Asian cultures have enjoyed tofu for millennia—with good reason: Tofu is low in fat, high in calcium and iron, and extremely versatile. Also called "bean curd" (it's made from soybeans and water), tofu is one of those magical ingredients that's like a blank canvas, as it takes on the flavors of whatever it's being cooked with. That means it allows you to create a vast range of edible masterpieces—from sweet desserts to savory main meals. The soft silken variety, typically sold in small aseptic bricks, lends itself to creamy "cheesecakes" and puddings, and with a food processor and a pinch of fresh herbs and spices, it's easily transformed into savory dips and spreads, too. Firm tofu tends to be the most agreeable for first-timers—especially the extra-firm nigari-style. It has none of the "wobble" that many tofu-phobes fear, and it maintains its structure in soups and stir-fries and on the grill. For next-level firmness that really mimics meat, freeze your tofu in its packaging, then thaw and press to remove any excess water before preparing.

Seitan

Seitan (*say*-tan) has earned the apt moniker "wheat meat" for its ultra-chewy texture, and is one of the most versatile plant foods available. Its origins are humble; it's essentially what's left after removing the starch and bran from standard-issue wheat flour. This stretchy, high-protein base is then combined with a liquid to form a sticky dough that's simmered, steamed,

Organics

We always recommend using organic ingredients whenever possible. Though we don't list "organic" in the ingredients list for every recipe here, supporting our local organic farmers is something near and dear to us. For guidelines on which fresh fruits and veggies are the most (and least!) pesticide-laden, check out the Dirty Dozen and Clean Fifteen (page 198). In our pantry, you'll always find as many organic products as possible. We encourage you to do the same.

or baked before being dressed and devoured. With the help of sauces and marinades, this chameleon of the faux-meat universe transforms into toothsome sausages, burgers, meatballs, and even "ribs" for the barbecue. While seitan is simple enough to prepare at home, it's even easier to visit your local natural foods store and choose among the prepackaged deli slices, miniature roasts, and seasoned chunks. In Asian grocery stores, it's commonly marketed as "vegetarian duck," and sold in cans beside the bamboo shoots and preserved vegetables.

Tempeh

A staple in Indonesian cuisine, tempeh—typically made from fermented whole soybeans—adds heft to traditional rice dishes, salads, satays, and curried stews. In Bali, you'll find street vendors selling deep-fried tempeh "chips" as a popular snack food. The flavor of plain tempeh falls on the earthy side and benefits from seasoning before, during, and after the cooking process. The smoked and preseasoned varieties can stand alone with a simple pinch of salt and some accompanying greens or grains. If you're transitioning to a meat-free diet and craving a BLT or Reuben, reach for one of the many packaged fake-bacon products made with tempeh. They're close enough to fill the smoky, salty void. An added selling point is tempeh's nutritional profile: It's loaded with trace minerals and probiotics that support a healthy immune system.

TAKE IT FROM ME

Kristin Bauer van Straten, *actress*

Are you vegan? I eat about 80 percent vegan, and 100 percent vegetarian.

What made you interested in cooking specifically vegan meals? I'm no cook, never have been, but I married an omnivore who *loves* to cook but couldn't figure out how to cook for me. So we started taking Spork Foods classes and we both love them, which says a lot because my husband won't sacrifice taste for any reason.

What's your favorite vegan dish to cook? If I am really doing it up it's the Spork risotto recipe; it's heavenly.

What vegan dish has surprised you the most? My husband was shocked at how every single recipe the ladies have taught us is tasty. He says, "I don't care what it is if it tastes this good!" A simple recipe was what turned him to the plant side: the Greek Lentil Salad.

What is the most useful tip you've learned about vegan cooking? To use the dull side of the knife after chopping to collect the food off the cutting board! Our knives were always dulling. Huge bit of info.

Sub In

It might seem like you're going to be buying a bunch of packages of vegan meats and cheeses when you start to mix up your menu with plant-based meals. But never fear, there are so very many options available these days, both in packaged and whole-food forms. Our recipes highlight our favorite subs for meat and dairy, but they are by no means an exhaustive list. Here are a few ideas for both easy grab-and-go packaged goodies and unprocessed, whole-food options.

CHICKEN

Gardein Chick'n Scallopini

Cook and slice onto salads, shred for tacos, or serve beside a pile of fluffy mashed potatoes.

Maitake Mushrooms

Also called "Hen of the Woods," these 'shrooms lend a chicken-like texture to enchiladas and veggie stir-fries.

GROUND BEEF

Beyond Meat Crumbles

Browning these chewy crumbles with onion and Mexican spices makes the perfect base for tacos.

Lentils

The humble lentil, when cooked, is a dead ringer for ground beef in Bolognese sauce or Sloppy Joes.

SAUSAGE

Tofurky Italian Sausage

Sliced thinly, it's pepperoni for your pizza. Straight off the grill and onto a bun, they trump any meat-based brat.

Nuts & 'Shrooms

For a hearty sausage flavor and toothsome texture, we love the combination of mushrooms and walnuts. Check out our Walnut Breakfast Sausages, page 41.

BACON

Lightlife Tempeh Bacon

Sizzle a few slices and sandwich between layers of juicy tomato and crisp lettuce and you've got an even better BLT.

Carrots

Wake up your mornings with a sizzling pan of … carrots! Long, thin strips of seasoned carrot make an excellent pig-free bacon.

PORK

Field Roast Celebration Loaf

This stuffed wheat-gluten loaf will remind you of Sunday dinners at Grandma's house.

Jackfruit

Season canned young jackfruit with a tomato-y barbecue sauce, and pulled-pork sandwiches are back on the menu.

FISH

Gardein Fish Filet

Fish-stick flavor without the fins and scales? It exists, and tastes even better than the frozen fish fingers from childhood.

Tempeh

A bit of mayo and chopped onion transforms steamed tempeh into a tuna salad facsimile that's divine heaped on toasted bread.

NARY A DAIRY

Why limit yourself to full-fat and 2% dairy milk when you can have chocolate-mint hazelnut, pumpkin-spice almond, and rich vanilla soy milks? The plant-based "dairy" universe is enormous, and continues to expand into exciting new territory. Aged cheeses, creamy bagel spreads, and cultured yogurts are the new nondairy norm. If you appreciate healthy variety that comes in endless flavors, you'll love experimenting with these animal milk alternatives.

Almond

Its mild, neutral flavor and light-bodied texture make almond milk ideal for drinking plain or as a base for a wide variety of recipes. It has curried favor with home cooks who appreciate how simple it is to make at home by just soaking almonds in purified water, while bakers value its affinity for and adaptability to conventional cake and sweetened bread recipes. Almond milk is also a coffeehouse favorite, since it's less prone to curdling in acidic coffee than soy. Besides milk, almonds are now transformed into rich cheeses and yogurts that are definitely worth exploring.

Cashew

Cashew milk is among the richest milks available, which makes it a good substitute in recipes calling for cream. Because it's low in naturally occurring sugars but high in vitamin E and the feel-good amino acid

TAKE IT FROM ME

Caroline MacDonald, *VP Sales & Marketing, along with husband* **Bob** *and daughter* **Casey**

Are you vegan? We are about 75 percent vegan, 25 percent vegetarian.

What made you interested in cooking specifically vegan meals? Our entire family adopted a plant-based diet for health benefits, and we wanted to expand our menus at home.

What's your favorite vegan dish to eat? Smoky collard greens, and for dessert, caramelized banana spring roll squares.

What is the most useful tip you've learned about vegan cooking? Using arrowroot for thickening soups and sauces, and making our own vanilla-flavored sugar.

called tryptophan, you might find yourself going back for seconds of whatever you've prepared with your cashew milk. Try making it at home by whizzing cashews, water, and pinch of salt and sugar in a blender, then pour onto cereal, into creamy sauces, or stir into a pot of mashed potatoes. Cashews are having a moment in the nut cheese trend, too, making appearances in cream cheese-style spreads and sturdier aged-style wheels.

Coconut

Not to be confused with the cream-on-top variety sold in cans, coconut milk beverages are sold in cartons alongside the other nondairy milks in the supermarket refrigerator case (and also in non-refrigerated aseptic cartons). Expect a neutral flavor with a hint of coconutty sweetness that adapts particularly well to dessert recipes. While coconut milk contains no protein, it does have a fair amount of fat, which lends a pleasantly creamy texture. After you've experimented with coconut milk on your oatmeal and in your pancake batter, move on to cultured coconut yogurt and some of the delectable coconut ice creams on the market.

Oat

In Scandinavia, oat milk is the beverage of choice in trendy cafés, supplanting soy and almond in the "alt" milk department. Why? It's sustainably produced, neutral in flavor, and interchangeable with dairy milk in coffee drinks. Oat milk boasts a high fiber content but is low in fat, and is a good source of naturally occurring beta-glucans, touted for their ability to lower potentially harmful blood cholesterol. Besides its nutritional edge, oat milk is the most affordable of all the nondairy milks when you make it at home, costing just pennies per serving.

Rice

Rice milk carries the distinction of being hypoallergenic, and thus a popular choice for people managing food allergies. Its mildly sweet flavor is developed during the production process, when the rice's natural carbohydrates turn to sugars. Light in texture and flavor, it's most comparable to low-fat dairy milk and can be used interchangeably in recipes that call for low-fat or 2% cow's milk. While not the best choice for creamy dishes, it's perfect on cereal or for making that cinnamon-infused Mexican specialty called *horchata*.

Soy

The OG of the plant-milk universe is also the most comparable to full-fat dairy milk in both texture and versatility. The "beany" flavor most palpable in plain varieties virtually vanishes in soups and sauces, and is totally masked in the vanilla flavors that work so well poured over hot and cold cereals or blended into smoothies. Soy milk boasts potent phytonutrients and protein equal to cow's milk, and costs less than almond, cashew, and many other milks. Keep your eyes peeled—and your palate prepared— for products made with soy milk including rich and decadent ice creams, yogurts, holiday nogs, and coffee creamers.

TAKE IT FROM US

Ari Solomon, *Director of Communications, Mercy For Animals* & **Mikko Alanne**, *Screenwriter/Producer*

Are you vegan? We've both been vegan for 10 years.

What made you interested in cooking specifically vegan meals? When we went vegan we expanded our horizons and experimented with foods we'd never tried before. We bought cookbooks and went to cooking classes. And it felt so good knowing that every meal we prepared was entirely cruelty-free!

What's your favorite vegan dish to cook? Ari's Syrian grandmother would make *mujadara*, which is basically lentils sautéed with caramelized onions served over rice. It's delicious! Mikko loves elaborate sauces, from herbed cashew creams to port wine balsamic glazes . . . you get the picture!

What is the most useful tip you've learned about vegan cooking? Use the side of a knife to crush garlic cloves to easily remove the skin.

TAKE IT FROM ME

Hayley Marie Norman, *actress and comedian*

Are you vegan? I'm just a few months shy of celebrating my eighth year as a vegan!

What made you interested in cooking specifically vegan meals? I've always been intimidated by the idea of cooking and frankly, as a single woman, couldn't think of anything more depressing than slaving in the kitchen over a vegan meal for one. But after taking a Spork class, I realized how fun, festive, and easy making tasty food could really be.

What's your favorite vegan dish to cook? One time I tried to win an ex-boyfriend back by mentioning I was making tacos. People love my tacos.

What is the most useful tip you've learned about vegan cooking? I thought I was going to be relegated to a life of watery tofu, but Jenny and Heather taught me the best way around that—by pressing it out!

Crazy Grab Bag

A few decades ago, powdered soy reconstituted in water was the only nondairy milk alternative widely available. Today, even small corner stores carry nondairy milk, and at well-stocked supermarkets and natural foods emporiums, there are dozens of options to choose from, including those made from pistachios (yes, it's green), hemp seeds (rich and loaded with omega-3 and -6 fatty acids), or a combination of hemp, cashew, and almond. The best way to decide which milk is right for you is to taste-test, or start experimenting at home with homemade varieties.

EGGSCHANGE

Aside from their ubiquitous presence at the breakfast table in the form of omelets, scrambles, and Hollandaise-topped Benedict, eggs play a discreet role in many of the foods we grew up eating. They function as binders and as leavening agents in muffins and breads, and they give structure to mayonnaise—yet eggs are in no way the only choice we have when preparing these familiar favorites. As these stand-ins suggest, the plant kingdom offers a bounty of egg-like options for whatever's on the menu. Experiment with these substitutes for a seamless transition to egg-free eating, from breakfast straight through to dessert.

The Small Stuff

And How To Not Sweat It

That old cliché, "It's the journey, not the destination," gets a fresh start when applied to those of us who are trying to incorporate more vegan options into our daily diets. On this trip, we can forget about perfection (hint: It doesn't exist!) and aim for "good enough," since this edible adventure is as much about the simple enjoyment of food as it is about the health, environmental, and animal-friendly perks that accompany it.

As you explore the vast and varied world of plant foods, try to imagine "success" in terms of the scope of your experiences: the more you dabble in new flavors, the more you "win." That might mean trying tempeh bacon instead of sausage with breakfast one day, replacing grilled cheese with avocado and roasted veggies on another, and using a creamy soy-based ice cream instead of a dairy one in your next homemade milkshake. These little "wins" will motivate you to keep branching out into unexplored territory and give your taste buds new terrain to tread.

As you begin incorporating more vegan meals into your diet, you'll discover quite a lot. For example, you might not have realized that gelatin lurks in your favorite candy until mid-chew, when you decide to read the fine print on the package, or that your beloved morning pastry gets its shiny veneer from an egg wash. All the little mysteries will reveal themselves in time, and it's important to cut yourself some slack so you don't feel overwhelmed by the tiny details.

Take time to celebrate each vegan "victory" and relish the meat-and-dairy-free dining experiences to come. To get you pumped for your next plant-based foray, consider choosing one recipe from this book to prepare, and inviting a friend over to help you cook. Having a culinary comrade will enhance the overall experience, and might even mean making two recipes instead of one.

Do I Have To...

Buy a complete set of new cookware?

Good news: That six-piece Le Creuset set you shelled out a week's wages for will adapt seamlessly to your new cooking habits. In place of pot roast, toss a colorful mélange of root vegetables into your fancy casserole pan. Instead of simmering a beef stew, whip up some blue ribbon chili with seitan. And put that skillet to use for egg-free Sunday pancakes instead of corned-beef hash. If you find yourself going wild for grains as you dive into plant-based cooking, you *might* consider investing in a rice cooker. Besides taking the hassle out of the rice-prep process, these handy contraptions can also be used to cook quinoa and other grains. Prices begin at about $30 for basic models, and often come with a steamer basket and other accessories that make preparing multiple dishes simultaneously a tasty possibility.

Eat at exclusively vegan restaurants?

Heck, no! More and more omnivorous restaurants are adding vegan items to their menus to satisfy mixed groups, Meatless Monday diners, and health-conscious eaters. Scout the menu for items with a "V" beside them, and don't be shy about asking your server for simple substitutions. Pizzas are easily prepared without cheese, tacos can be stuffed with beans and guacamole, and pasta dressed with a rich pomodoro sauce and served with a green salad is easy-peasy for kitchen staff to prepare. Nabbed reservations at a Michelin-starred spot? Call the restaurant in advance and ask what the chef can create for you. Kitchen pros love a challenge, and this affords them the opportunity to break out of culinary routines. Ethnic restaurants, too, are havens for hungry herbivores; be bold and branch out! Ethiopian dishes served with spongy injera, Chinese dim sum stuffed with mustard greens and glass noodles, and spicy Malaysian laksa soups brimming with fresh vegetables and piquant spices await.

Resign myself to a life devoid of flavor and joy?

On the contrary! Many of us don't even realize we're in a food rut until we decide to shake things up. When we break from our usual habits and routines, we tend to replace them with novel foods that we'd never have considered otherwise, for example, tempeh or shiitake mushrooms. Dabbling in new food terrain lights up the part of our brains that makes us feel good by releasing dopamine into our systems, which actually supports continued culinary adventure-seeking. Dare to explore Middle Eastern or Latin markets and see what za'atar and chipotles are all about; move beyond curiosity and actually buy those mysterious microgreens you've been eyeing at the farmers' market; or do some impulse shopping in the vegan dairy aisle and toss a tub of cultured coconut yogurt into your basket. Challenging yourself by trying new things—and discovering you actually enjoy them—is definitely the opposite of bland, and might even be the epitome of joy.

Give up my dreams of becoming a world-champion athlete?

Have you heard of David Carter? He's a 300-pound NFL champ crushing it on a vegan diet. Ditto for ultra-endurance athlete Rich Roll, and tennis star Venus Williams. It's no secret that vegan diets can actually *improve* performance rather than hinder it, by fueling our bodies with lean, clean energy. The key to maintaining health and fitness on a plant-based diet is to avoid the junk-food vegan trap. French fries, potato chips, and soft drinks are all vegan, but you'll never win any medals for athletic prowess if those form the foundation of your diet. Load up on healthy carbs, fresh vegetables and fruits, and meaty beans, and prepare to take home nutritional gold.

Learn completely new cooking skills?

If you can stir a pot of soup, chop vegetables, make a sandwich, or flip a burger, you've nailed the "secrets" of vegan food prep—essentially the same skills you'd use to prepare animal-based meals. Cooking classes are a fun way to expand one's culinary skills (wink, wink), but if you don't have the time or access, you can still master your vegan cooking skills. If you've always wanted to learn how to bake bread, roll sushi, or master a spicy Thai curry, there's a class to meet your needs and desires, but keep in mind that good cookbooks (like this one), and a sense of adventure will take you far and keep you full.

For Scrambles, Try Extra-Firm Tofu

Since the dawn of the packaged tofu era, everyone from college-dorm cooks to professional chefs have been turning out tasty scrambles using extra-firm tofu. Why extra firm? It can stand up to the mushrooms, onions, spinach, and peppers you toss into your skillet, and it yields a definite scrambled-egg texture. When topped with salsa or your favorite enchilada sauce, your Mexican scramble takes a leap to the next level.

For Omelets, Try the VeganEgg

The folks at Follow Your Heart are food pioneers, bringing the world its first widely available eggless mayonnaise and one of the first melty dairy-free cheeses. When the company released its first faux-egg product, a collective cheer could be heard roaring out from kitchens around the globe. The VeganEgg is made from a surprise ingredient—seaweed—and makes an omelet that rivals anything you'd order off a roadside diner menu. Just like eggs, the VeganEgg starts out a liquid and then solidifies during the cooking process. If you're more of a frittata fan than an omelet eater, this little dynamo works wonders under a broiler, too.

But What About...

Protein?

Often overlooked fact: All plants contain protein. Yup—all of 'em! Some offer more of these muscle-building amino acid chains than others, but you just need to look at the big herbivores of the animal kingdom—cows, elephants, and gorillas, for starters—to see that eating plants and getting sufficient protein are not mutually exclusive. The key to optimal protein intake is simply to eat a variety of plant foods; integrate grains, beans, and greens into most of your meals and you're good to go.

Eating Too Much Soy?

When it comes right down to it, soy is, well, just a bean. Like other beans, it's loaded with nutritional value, including protein, iron, and calcium. For anyone consuming a balanced diet full of grains, beans, fruits, and vegetables, there's no need to fear overconsumption. When in doubt, purchase only organic soy products.

Iron?

Iron is necessary for building healthy red blood cells, and is easily found in a wide variety of foods you likely already consume such as quinoa, kale, apricots, and kidney beans. The iron in leafy greens like chard and kale can be more easily absorbed by adding a squeeze of lemon juice before serving, and using a cast iron pan to fry up your veggie burgers will also impart an iron boost.

Calcium?

One myth many of us were raised on is the one about dairy being our best source of calcium. Plants, as it happens, are even better sources, since the body absorbs calcium from plants more easily than calcium from animal-derived sources. To keep your bones healthy and strong, explore the wonderful world of dark, leafy greens—chard, kale, collards, broccoli—and find creative ways to pair them with another solid source of calcium: beans. Black beans, soybeans, and white kidney beans are just a few of the hearty, nutritious options.

B_{12}?

Back when we all lived in less industrialized, more agrarian societies, getting sufficient B_{12} was easy. The soil was rich with it and we'd ingest it—and a spectrum of other vitamins and minerals—via the dirt remnants clinging to our carrots and potatoes. Today's intensive agricultural practices have stripped the earth of its naturally occurring vitamins, so supplementing with B_{12} is recommended for those avoiding eggs, dairy, meat, and fish. Easy ways to meet your health needs include taking a vitamin supplement and eating fortified cereals and nondairy milks. Or, do like the British and make Marmite spread a part of your daily dining routine.

For Baking,
Try Flaxseed

One long-standing vegan baker's hack is to add a couple tablespoons of flax meal to the dry ingredients of any baking recipe. (In this book, you'll notice that many of our recipes call to follow this method.) Another option is to combine these two ingredients and let the mixture sit for 10 minutes. The result of this kitchen chemistry exercise is a clear, viscous liquid that bears an uncanny resemblance to egg whites, and can be used the same way in recipes that call for an egg binder. Try it in muffins, breads, and cupcake batter.

For Egg Salad,
Try Silken Tofu

Silken tofu's texture is a dead ringer for a soft-boiled egg white, so it follows that with a bit of mayo, minced onion, and—what the heck, go nuts—some chopped pickle or olives, you'd have yourself a pretty accurate eggless approximation of traditional egg salad. For that added bit of egginess, try adding a pinch of *kala namak*—a sulfuric salt easily procured at Indian markets or online. Kala namak is also sometimes called black salt but don't be fooled by the misnomer—it's actually light pink in color.

TAKE IT FROM ME

Jackie Johnson, *Actor/Comedian*

Are you vegan? Yes.

What made you interested in cooking specifically vegan meals? I went vegan cold turkey after deciding it was the right thing to do. Then I found myself eating a lot of what most people would consider "side dishes." I wanted well-rounded, full meal options that are relatively foolproof to make at home, so I started to educate myself on how to do that.

What vegan dish has surprised you the most? Jackfruit! I couldn't believe how similar the texture and flavor is to a BBQ sandwich from my meat-eating days.

What is the most useful tip you've learned about vegan cooking? It's all about creating flavor profiles that satisfy you. With the right spices, herbs, and techniques you can get anything to taste rich and yummy. I know what flavors I like now and how to get pretty much any plant-based dish to taste hearty and savory. Nutritional yeast is kind of my best friend.

TAKE IT FROM ME

Bob Goldberg, *Co-founder,*
Follow Your Heart/Earth Island

Are you vegan? After being a vegetarian for about 40 years, I turned vegan about 4 years ago.

What made you interested in cooking specifically vegan meals? Hunger. Seriously, it was the way I felt, not so much physically, but the way it made me feel about myself and my place in the world.

What's your favorite vegan dish to eat? I'll take some fresh-picked berries any day over just about anything.

What is the most useful tip you've learned about vegan cooking? The Spork sisters had a great tip for preparing tempeh. Steaming it before adding it to a dish minimizes the bitterness that is sometimes associated with tempeh.

What vegan dish has surprised you the most? We made a fresh "egg" pasta, using VeganEgg, formed it into tortelloni, and stuffed it with a sun-dried tomato–cashew cheese we learned from the Spork Sisters. Mamma mia!!!

CHEESE, INTERRUPTED

Casomorphins. Haven't heard of them? Then you probably aren't aware of the role they play in our collective love affair with cheese. The protein fragments—which have a structure alarmingly similar to that of opiates—unfold in your digestive system to incite crave-inducing pleasure. While nondairy cheeses can't offer you the same addictive properties that casomorphins do, they *can* offer creamy, stretchy, luscious opportunities to fulfill all your cheese-y desires.

For Pizza, Try Shreds

Do you prefer your pies smothered in a gooey, über-melty layer of cheese? Then you're going to love shred-style vegan options. The packaged shreds deliver authentic pizzeria-style goodness that bubbles and goes golden in the oven. This is your go-to for not just pizzas, but enchiladas, nachos, and lasagna, too.

For Sandwiches, Try Slices

The thicker cut and smooth texture of slices is perfect in sammies both hot and cold. Stuff a few slices into a baguette with tomato, onion, and a drizzle of vinaigrette, and you've got a simple, tasty submarine sandwich. Melt it between two slices of bread and you'll be back in the land of luscious grilled cheese.

Oh, Oil!

We recommend using neutral-tasting oil in the majority of our recipes. We like safflower and grapeseed oils because they have a neutral flavor, so what you taste is actually the delicious dish, and not just the oil in which it was cooked! If you prefer to use regular vegetable, refined coconut, or canola oil, those work, too. It's important to avoid cooking at high temperatures with olive and sesame oils since they can easily turn carcinogenic when heated too high.

For Baguettes, Try Spreadable Cashew Cheeses

Nothing says "picnic" in quite the same way as a crusty baguette slathered in a creamy, spreadable cheese. For the ultimate summer alfresco dining experience, grab your favorite bread, a tub of whatever flavor grabs your fancy—versions with chives or black pepper are especially tasty—and head outside! Almost every grocery store these days offers at least one version of cashew goodness.

For Cheese Plates, Try Aged Cashew or Almond Cheese

These elegant artisan wheels look right at home alongside a plate of traditional Brie and Camembert, and have been known to appeal to even the most dairy-oriented palates. The price tag on these bad boys usually reflects their artisanal status, but they're perfect for special occasions.

For Topping, Try Nutritional Yeast

When presented with a plate of pasta pomodoro, an instant reflex for many of us is to reach for a shaker of Parmesan cheese. If that sounds like you, now is the time to get acquainted with nutritional yeast. Despite its unfortunate name, this bulk-bin staple adds a rich, umami flavor to your dishes. You can toss it straight onto your pasta, or pulse in a food processor in equal parts with walnuts and a good grind of salt for a deeper flavor. Don't limit yourself to a mere sprinkle atop your spaghetti; shake it over pizza, popcorn, and salads, too. Warning: You may be tempted to eat this by the handful. (We've been there.)

Recipe
p.44

Breakfasts

The recipes in this chapter make breakfast fun to eat every day of the week, not just on weekends. From the quick and easy, like our Fig, Walnut, and Vegan Honey Breakfast Tartine (page 44), to the more decadent, like our Sautéed Kale Benedict with Hollandaise Sauce (page 47), rest assured, all of these dishes have been streamlined to cook in a snap. So go ahead: dive into this chapter for inspired mornings every day. Your days of grabbing a banana and heading out the door are numbered.

Vegan Sausage, Herb, and Cheese Tofu Scramble

NUT-FREE • **30 MINUTES OR LESS**

Serves 4

Prep time: 7 minutes

Cook time: 8 minutes

2 teaspoons vegan butter

1 (14-ounce) container extra-firm tofu, drained and pressed

2 teaspoons brown rice syrup

2 teaspoons light miso paste

2 tablespoons freshly squeezed lemon juice

¼ teaspoon sea salt

¼ teaspoon freshly ground black pepper

¼ teaspoon ground turmeric

¼ teaspoon garlic powder

2 to 4 vegan breakfast sausage patties, diced

2 tablespoons fresh chives, finely chopped

2 tablespoons fresh basil, finely chopped

¼ cup shredded vegan smoked Gouda or mozzarella cheese

The key to a delicious tofu scramble is lots of goodies. We like to theme it out with scrambles using Asian, Mexican, Mediterranean, or Southwest flavors. This is the perfect dish to experiment with and customize, so check out our variations, and remember—your own travels are also a great place to find inspiration.

1. Heat a skillet over medium heat. Add butter.

2. Into a mixing bowl, crumble tofu with hands. Add brown rice syrup, miso, and lemon juice and stir to incorporate. Add sea salt, pepper, turmeric, and garlic powder.

3. Transfer tofu mixture to skillet. Add sausage and cook for 1 to 2 minutes until beginning to brown. Cook for 3 to 5 minutes, or until golden.

4. Add chives and basil. Stir. Add cheese and stir well for 30 seconds to 1 minute to melt cheese. Remove from heat.

5. Serve garnished with additional chives and basil if desired and season to taste with sea salt and pepper.

TIP Press tofu stored in water by removing it from the container and placing it on a cooling rack over a plate to collect water. Top it with a weight, such as a lid from a heavy pan, or a large can. Leave it alone for about 10 minutes.

Variations

Here are some fun ways to change up the flavors of your scramble.

Southwest Tofu Scramble

½ cup cooked black beans
⅓ cup fresh or frozen (thawed) corn kernels
¼ teaspoon chipotle powder
¼ cup shredded vegan Pepper Jack cheese

Follow the original recipe as written through step 2. After transferring tofu mixture to skillet, substitute beans, corn, and chipotle powder for sausage and cook 3 to 5 minutes, until warmed through. Substitute Pepper Jack for Gouda and stir well for 30 seconds to 1 minute to melt cheese. Continue to follow original recipe as written, garnishing with herbs and seasoning to taste.

Mediterranean Tofu Scramble

¼ cup sun-dried tomatoes in oil, finely diced
2 tablespoons pitted Kalamata olives, diced
½ cup packed baby spinach
6 to 8 fresh basil leaves, coarsely chopped
¼ cup shredded vegan provolone cheese (optional)

Follow the original recipe as written through step 2. After transferring the tofu mixture to a skillet, substitute tomatoes, olives, and spinach for sausage and cook 2 to 4 minutes, until spinach is wilted. Add basil. Stir. Substitute provolone for Gouda (if using) and stir well for 30 seconds to 1 minute to melt cheese. Continue to follow original recipe as written, garnishing with herbs and seasoning to taste.

Asian Tofu Scramble

4 to 5 shiitake mushrooms, stemmed and cut into thin strips
2 teaspoons tamari or soy sauce (instead of sea salt)
2 teaspoons pickled ginger, finely chopped
¼ cup scallions, thinly sliced
2 teaspoons toasted sesame seeds

Follow the original recipe as written through step 2. After transferring the tofu mixture to a skillet, substitute mushrooms, tamari or soy sauce, and ginger for sausage and cook 3 to 5 minutes, until mushrooms give off their liquids and are tender. Add scallions and sesame seeds. Stir. Continue to follow original recipe, garnishing with herbs and seasoning to taste.

Almond Butter and Jelly-Stuffed French Toast

30 MINUTES OR LESS
Serves 4 to 6
Prep time: 10 minutes
Cook time: 10 minutes

½ cup whole-wheat pastry flour

2 tablespoons unbleached all-purpose flour

1 teaspoon aluminum-free baking powder

1½ teaspoons ground flaxseed

¼ teaspoon sea salt

3 tablespoons maple syrup

1 teaspoon vanilla extract

¾ cup unsweetened almond milk

2 tablespoons neutral-tasting oil, divided

6 tablespoons strawberry jelly

6 tablespoons almond butter

6 slices vegan sourdough bread

PB&Js are a lunchbox classic for a good reason. They're nourishing, quick to throw together, and tradeable in any lunchroom. We've shaken things up by using almond butter in our French toast version, kicking this "teacher's pet" up to a whole new level of yumminess.

1. In a medium bowl, whisk together flours, baking powder, flaxseed, and sea salt. Add maple syrup, vanilla, almond milk, and 1 tablespoon oil. Whisk batter until smooth. Do not over mix.

2. Preheat griddle or large nonstick pan to medium heat. Brush griddle or pan with remaining 1 tablespoon oil.

3. Spread 2 tablespoons jelly onto 3 slices of bread and 2 tablespoons almond butter onto the remaining 3 slices of bread. Top the jellied side of the bread with the almond butter side, making 3 sandwiches. Coat each sandwich in batter and then place on griddle or pan.

4. Cook over medium heat for about 5 minutes, or until bottom is slightly golden and edges look dry. Flip and cook for another 3 to 4 minutes, or until golden. If bread is thick, stand sandwich vertically in pan and cook 1 minute. This helps seal French toast.

TIP Don't forget to buy flaxseed ground, instead of whole, for ease of use. Store in the refrigerator or it will go bad in about one week's time.

Maple Coconut Granola

GLUTEN-FREE
30 MINUTES OR LESS

Makes 2¾ cups granola

Prep time: 8 minutes

Cook time: 20 minutes

3 tablespoons neutral-tasting oil, divided

2 cups gluten-free rolled oats

2 teaspoons vanilla extract

½ teaspoon coconut extract

½ teaspoon ground cinnamon

¼ teaspoon sea salt

3 tablespoons maple syrup

1 tablespoon brown rice syrup

½ cup large coconut flakes

⅓ cup almonds or pecans, coarsely chopped

Maple + coconut + oats = delicious homemade granola (calculator not required). Though simple, granola translates to multiple breakfast variations like parfaits, cereals served with nondairy milk, a companion to your favorite vegan yogurt, or on its own, by the handful.

1. Preheat oven to 350°F. Grease a baking sheet with 1 tablespoon oil.

2. In a medium bowl, combine oats, vanilla, coconut extract, cinnamon, sea salt, maple syrup and brown rice syrup, and remaining 2 tablespoons oil. Coat evenly. Add coconut flakes and nuts.

3. Spread mixture in an even layer on baking sheet.

4. Bake for 10 minutes, then stir, bringing granola at the edges toward the center. Repeat every 5 minutes, until the mixture has baked for about 20 minutes. Moving granola around during baking prevents burning.

TIP The granola can keep for up to 1 week if stored in an airtight container in the refrigerator.

Apple Coffee Cake Muffins

Makes 12 muffins
Prep time: 10 minutes
Cook time: 28 to 30 minutes

Breakfast and dessert have a lot of crossover, and coffee cake epitomizes this convergence. To make these muffins acceptable as a morning meal, we snuck in fiber with the fresh apples and protein with the walnuts.

FOR THE TOPPING

¼ cup evaporated cane sugar
¼ cup toasted walnuts, chopped
1 tablespoon vegan butter
1 tablespoon whole-wheat pastry flour
⅛ teaspoon ground cinnamon
⅛ teaspoon sea salt

FOR THE MUFFIN BATTER

½ cup vegan butter,
  at room temperature
½ cup evaporated cane sugar
¾ cup vegan sour cream
3 tablespoons unsweetened
  almond milk
2 tablespoons maple syrup
1 teaspoon vanilla extract
1 cup unbleached all-purpose flour
½ cup whole-wheat pastry flour
1 teaspoon aluminum-free
  baking powder
½ teaspoon baking soda
¼ teaspoon sea salt
1 tablespoon ground flaxseed
1 teaspoon apple cider vinegar
1 Pink Lady or Gala apple,
  peeled, cored, and finely diced
  (1½ cups)

Preheat oven to 350°F, line 12 muffin cups, and lightly grease the liners.

TO PREPARE THE TOPPING

Pulse sugar, walnuts, butter, flour, cinnamon, and sea salt in a food processor, or mix by hand. Set aside.

TO PREPARE THE BATTER

1.   In a large mixing bowl, the bowl of a stand mixer, or using a handheld mixer, cream together butter and sugar. Add sour cream, almond milk, maple syrup, and vanilla and whisk until uniform.

2.   In a large bowl, combine flours, baking powder, baking soda, sea salt, and flaxseed. Whisk to incorporate.

3.   Add dry ingredients to creamed mixture and whisk until smooth. Add vinegar and whisk. Fold in apples.

4.   Spoon batter into cups of muffin pan, about ⅓ cup batter per muffin. Sprinkle about 2 teaspoons topping over each muffin. Bake for 30 to 32 minutes, or until a toothpick comes out clean.

TIP   Chop the apples (or any fruit for that matter) on a cutting board used solely for fruit or dessert. This prevents mingling the flavors of your fruit with the unwanted tastes of foods like garlic and onion.

TIP   The tops of the muffins will get crunchy, so when cooled, run a small knife around the edges to loosen them easily from the pan.

Blueberry Tofu Ricotta Pancakes

Makes about 8 (3-inch) pancakes

Prep time: 10 minutes

Cook time: 8 minutes

FOR THE RICOTTA

¼ cup raw or toasted cashews

⅓ cup water

½ (14-ounce) container extra-firm tofu, drained and pressed

1 tablespoon freshly squeezed lemon juice

1 teaspoon evaporated cane sugar

¼ teaspoon sea salt

Pinch freshly grated nutmeg

1 teaspoon neutral-tasting oil

FOR THE PANCAKE BATTER

¾ cup unbleached all-purpose flour

1 tablespoon evaporated cane sugar

1 teaspoon aluminum-free baking powder

¼ teaspoon ground cinnamon

¼ teaspoon sea salt

½ cup unsweetened almond milk

1 teaspoon vanilla extract

1 teaspoon neutral-tasting oil

½ cup fresh blueberries

1 to 2 teaspoons vegan butter

Multiple-choice question: When is it appropriate to eat pancakes? For:

a) Breakfast

b) Lunch

c) Dinner

d) All of the above

If you guessed "d," you passed! Pancakes are good on their own, but when you make homemade ricotta and throw in ripe blueberries, breakfast, lunch, or dinner gets that much better.

TO PREPARE THE RICOTTA

1. In a blender or food processor, add cashews and water. Blend until smooth. Set aside.

2. Into a large bowl, crumble tofu with your hands. Add lemon juice, sugar, sea salt, nutmeg, and oil. Add cashew mixture. Mix together well. Set aside to develop flavors.

TO PREPARE THE PANCAKE BATTER

In a large bowl, whisk together flour, sugar, baking powder, cinnamon, and sea salt. Add almond milk, vanilla, and oil. Fold in ricotta mixture. Once uniform, fold in blueberries.

Heat a large griddle over medium heat and add butter. Ladle about ¼ cup batter onto griddle, giving pancakes room to spread. Cook pancakes about 4 minutes per side, until golden.

TIP To make a savory ricotta variation, simply eliminate the cane sugar and replace the sweetness with 2 teaspoons miso paste, ¼ teaspoon garlic powder, and ¼ teaspoon freshly ground black pepper. Use in any application that calls for ricotta.

Creamy Coconut Chia Pudding with Raspberry Coulis

GLUTEN-FREE

Serves 4 to 6

Prep time: 10 to 15 minutes

Chilling time: 2 hours to overnight

FOR THE CHIA PUDDING

1 (13.5-ounce) can full-fat coconut milk

1 cup unsweetened almond milk

3 tablespoons maple syrup

1 tablespoon evaporated cane sugar

1 teaspoon vanilla extract

¼ teaspoon sea salt

⅓ cup black chia seeds

FOR THE RASPBERRY COULIS

¼ cup evaporated cane sugar

1 tablespoon water

6 ounces fresh raspberries,
   rinsed and patted dry

½ teaspoon Cointreau

⅛ teaspoon sea salt

2 tablespoons flaked coconut,
   for topping (optional)

TIP When you're first whisking this recipe, it may seem like the liquid-to-chia seed ratio is high. But be patient, as those small but mighty chia seeds will drink it all up.

Chia pudding and homework have one very important trait in common—both are best completed in the evening in preparation for the day ahead. Soak chia seeds in rich coconut milk the night before you make this dish. Overnight, they'll drink up and expand, developing a wonderful flavor and texture. The raspberry coulis lends a tartness that won't disappoint.

TO PREPARE THE PUDDING

1. In a mixing bowl, combine coconut milk, almond milk, maple syrup, sugar, vanilla, and sea salt. Whisk until uniform. Add chia seeds and whisk again until uniform.

2. Let mixture rest for 5 to 10 minutes and then stir once more to break up any lumps. Cover and let rest in refrigerator for 2 hours to overnight.

TO PREPARE THE COULIS

1. Heat a small pot over medium heat and add sugar and water. Whisk. Bring to a simmer and add raspberries. Cook 1 to 2 minutes, stirring constantly, to soften raspberries. Remove from heat and set aside.

2. Add raspberry mixture into a blender with Cointreau and sea salt and blend on high about 15 seconds, or until smooth. Strain mixture through a fine-mesh strainer into a bowl, using a spatula to help move mixture through strainer. Set aside until ready to use. Mixture holds in refrigerator for up to 3 days.

3. To serve, scoop pudding into individual glasses and top with coulis and flaked coconut (if using).

Ultimate Breakfast Sandwich with Secret Sauce

NUT-FREE • **30 MINUTES OR LESS**

Makes 6 sandwiches

Prep time: 12 minutes

Cook time: 10 minutes

FOR THE TOFU EGG

1 (14-ounce) container extra-firm tofu, drained and pressed

2 teaspoons freshly squeezed lemon juice

¼ teaspoon sea salt

¼ teaspoon freshly ground black pepper

¼ teaspoon ground turmeric

2 teaspoons vegan butter

FOR THE SECRET SAUCE

3 tablespoons ketchup

3 tablespoons vegan mayonnaise

1 teaspoon freshly squeezed lemon juice

1 teaspoon maple syrup

1 tablespoon nutritional yeast

⅛ teaspoon sea salt

⅛ teaspoon freshly ground black pepper

6 vegan English muffins, split

6 slices vegan American cheese

1 tomato, cut into ¼-inch-thick rounds

1 avocado, peeled and cut into thin strips

The morning after Thanksgiving, instead of eating leftovers as they are, our family piles into the kitchen to make and devour these breakfast sammies. They're so darn good, you'll forget about how full you were the day before. Yes, we are *really* giving away our secret sauce recipe, because we're really bad at keeping secrets . . . and we think you'll love it.

TO PREPARE THE TOFU EGG

Cut tofu block in half and cut into 6 (¼-inch-thick) rectangles. Place tofu on a plate and drizzle both sides of tofu with lemon juice, sea salt, and pepper and sprinkle with turmeric. Heat a griddle over medium heat and add butter. Cook tofu for 3 to 4 minutes per side, or until golden. Set aside.

TO PREPARE THE SECRET SAUCE

1. In a bowl, whisk together ketchup, mayonnaise, lemon juice, maple syrup, nutritional yeast, sea salt, and pepper until uniform. Set aside.

2. Top split side of 1 English muffin with 1 slice cheese. Toast in toaster oven for 5 to 7 minutes, or until golden. Spread secret sauce on split side of bare muffin half.

3. Place 1 piece tofu, 1 slice tomato, and a few avocado slices on top of cheesy side. Top with secret sauce muffin side. Repeat for all sandwiches. Serve warm.

TIP If you love tofu as much as we do, you may want to invest in a tofu press, which presses out the water so you can let the flavor in. Our favorite is the TofuXpress.

Oven-Roasted Sweet Potato and Tempeh Bacon Hash

NUT-FREE

Serves 4 to 6
Prep time: 15 minutes
Cook time: 35 minutes

1 sweet potato, diced (about 3 cups)

1 russet potato, diced (about 1½ cups)

½ red bell pepper, finely chopped

½ yellow onion, diced

1 clove garlic, finely chopped

6 strips tempeh bacon, coarsely chopped

2 tablespoons neutral-tasting oil

½ teaspoon dried basil

½ teaspoon dried oregano

¼ teaspoon sea salt

¼ teaspoon freshly ground black pepper

2 teaspoons maple syrup

1 tablespoon stone-ground mustard

2 tablespoons freshly squeezed lemon juice, divided

1 tablespoon fresh rosemary, stemmed and finely chopped

If you find chopping up veggies as therapeutic as we do, this breakfast is perfect for your mind and body. If not, no worries; just say this mantra the whole time: "lots of chopping, maximum taste." This dish is deeply satisfying, hearty, and keeps well throughout the week. You can even use it as a side dish at dinner. All that chopping will be well worth your while.

1. Preheat oven to 375°F.

2. On a large baking sheet, combine sweet potato, potato, bell pepper, onion, garlic, and tempeh bacon. Toss with oil to coat. Add basil, oregano, sea salt, pepper, maple syrup, mustard, 1 tablespoon lemon juice, and rosemary. Mix to incorporate.

3. Roast for 32 to 35 minutes, depending on size of dice, or until a fork easily pierces a piece of potato or sweet potato.

4. Add remaining 1 tablespoon lemon juice and serve warm.

 **TIP** To reheat, pop it in a 375°F oven for 7 to 10 minutes.

Walnut Breakfast Sausages

30 MINUTES OR LESS

Makes about 8
(2-inch round) sausages

Prep time: 8 minutes

Cook time: 13 minutes

1 tablespoon vegan butter

½ white onion, finely diced

2 cloves garlic, finely chopped

6 to 8 cremini mushrooms, diced

1 cup toasted walnut pieces

2 tablespoons freshly squeezed
lemon juice

2 tablespoons maple syrup

2 teaspoons red wine vinegar

1 teaspoon vegan
Worcestershire sauce

½ teaspoon sea salt

¼ teaspoon freshly ground
black pepper

½ teaspoon red pepper flakes

¼ teaspoon dried poultry
seasoning blend

1 teaspoon fennel seeds

⅓ cup almond meal

⅓ cup unbleached all-purpose flour

2 teaspoons neutral-tasting oil

Can you buy vegan sausages at the store? Yes. Then is it worth making your own? When they're this tasty, absolutely. While you're prepping your ingredients and whirling them around in your food processor, they won't look like sausages at first. Take a breath, be patient, and let the magic happen. Once they hit the skillet, the sausages really come together.

1. Heat a large sauté pan over medium-high heat and melt butter. Add onion and garlic and cook 3 to 5 minutes, or until softened. Add mushrooms and continue to cook 4 to 5 minutes. Set aside.

2. In a food processor or high-powered blender, combine walnuts, mushroom mixture, lemon juice, maple syrup, vinegar, Worcestershire sauce, sea salt, black pepper, red pepper flakes, poultry seasoning blend, fennel seeds, almond meal, and flour. Pulse until mixture is uniform but not perfectly smooth, about 20 pulses.

3. Heat a large sauté pan over medium heat and add oil. Scoop out mixture with a 1½-ounce ice cream scoop and place into pan, flattening slightly.

4. Cook for 3 to 4 minutes on each side, or until well browned. The texture will be crisp on the edges and slightly softer in the middle.

TIP For best results, use a nonstick skillet to cook up these li'l darlings.

Savory Cheddar and Basil Scones

Makes 8 to 10 (4-inch) scones
Prep time: 15 minutes
Cook time: 18 to 20 minutes

2½ cups unbleached all-purpose flour
1 tablespoon aluminum-free
  baking powder
1 tablespoon evaporated cane sugar
2 teaspoons ground flaxseed
½ teaspoon sea salt
½ teaspoon freshly ground
  black pepper
¼ teaspoon garlic powder
½ cup vegan butter
½ cup unsweetened almond
  or soy milk
¼ cup freshly squeezed lemon juice
8 to 10 fresh basil leaves, finely
  chopped
1 cup grated vegan Cheddar
  cheese, divided
1 teaspoon dried basil, for topping

TIP Don't overwork your dough; incorporate all ingredients until they are uniformly mixed, but no longer. If you overmix, you'll get a tough scone.

You'll probably be making these for breakfast, but since you will have some leftovers, it is our duty to tell you that they double as a delicious midnight snack as well. Fresh basil combined with the richness of Cheddar cheese makes these scones irresistible. If you have a pizza stone, definitely use it for these scones. It will give them a great crunch on the bottom, while still retaining a fluffy interior.

1. Preheat oven to 425°F. If using a pizza stone, add to oven while preheating.

2. In a large bowl, combine flour, baking powder, sugar, flaxseed, sea salt, pepper, and garlic powder. Whisk with a pastry cutter to incorporate.

3. Cut butter into mixture with pastry cutter until mixture appears crumbly.

4. Add almond or soy milk, lemon juice, fresh basil, and ¾ cup Cheddar. Mix until just incorporated. Dough will not be completely smooth.

5. Gather dough into a ball and place on a lightly floured surface. Roll dough into ½-inch-thick square. Cut into triangles of desired size.

6. Place scones on a baking sheet or floured surface (if using pizza stone) and top with dried basil and remaining ¼ cup Cheddar. If baking on a pizza stone, carefully transfer scones to hot pizza stone when ready to bake.

7. Bake for 18 to 20 minutes, or until golden brown.

Fig, Walnut, and Vegan Honey Breakfast Tartine

30 MINUTES OR LESS

Serves 4 to 6

Prep time: 5 minutes

Cook time: 2 minutes

4 to 6 thick slices fresh bread

4 to 6 fresh figs

½ cup vegan cream cheese

½ cup toasted walnuts, coarsely chopped

2 tablespoons vegan honey

¼ teaspoon sea salt

1 teaspoon freshly squeezed lemon juice, plus zest of ½ lemon

Eating figs feels like a spiritual experience to us, because our ancestors also enjoyed the very same delicacy thousands of years ago. Combining figs with walnuts and vegan honey piled atop freshly toasted bread takes this versatile fruit to a whole other transcendental plane.

1. In toaster oven, toast bread about 2 minutes, or until golden.

2. Meanwhile, slice figs into thin rounds. Set aside.

3. Slather each piece of toast generously with cream cheese. Add sliced figs, and sprinkle each piece with toasted walnuts. Drizzle with honey.

4. Sprinkle with sea salt, followed by lemon juice and zest.

TIP If you can't find vegan honey, whisk together 1 tablespoon brown rice syrup with 1 tablespoon agave. It works like a charm!

TIP Be sure to purchase fresh figs only one to two days before making this dish. They go bad quickly.

Ginger-Chocolate-Hazelnut Spread

GLUTEN-FREE
30 MINUTES OR LESS
Makes about 1 cup
Prep time: 3 minutes
Cook time: 7 minutes

1 cup whole raw hazelnuts

3 tablespoons coconut sugar
  or evaporated cane sugar

2 tablespoons unsweetened
  cocoa powder

2 tablespoons maple syrup

½ teaspoon vanilla extract

⅛ teaspoon sea salt

¼ cup soy milk creamer

1 tablespoon neutral-tasting oil

1 tablespoon fresh ginger, finely grated

¼ cup candied ginger,
  coarsely chopped

2 slices toasted bread (optional)

1 pint fresh berries, washed and
  patted dry (optional)

Hazelnut spreads are all the rage these days, and this easy homemade version gives you an excuse to eat chocolate before noon—if you actually need one. Like the Europeans who invented it, we spread this on everything—toast, bagels, pancakes, waffles, fruit—or just eat it by the spoonful.

1. Preheat oven to 350°F.

2. Place hazelnuts on a baking sheet and toast for 5 to 7 minutes, or until fragrant.

3. Place hazelnuts in food processor or high-powered blender. Add sugar, cocoa powder, maple syrup, vanilla, sea salt, creamer, oil, and fresh ginger. Process until smooth.

4. Serve topped with candied ginger. Or serve spread on toast and topped with fresh berries (if using).

TIP If you're only planning on purchasing a small amount of hazelnuts, or any nut for that matter, definitely shop in the bulk bin at your local grocery store. You can always freeze nuts to keep them around longer. Wildwood makes our preferred soy creamer. It has a more neutral flavor, and is less sweet than other creamers on the market.

Sautéed Kale Benedict with Hollandaise Sauce

Serves 4 to 6
(makes 1½ cups sauce)
Prep time: 20 minutes
Cook time: 20 minutes

FOR THE KALE BENEDICT

2 teaspoons neutral-tasting oil

1 bunch kale, stemmed and coarsely chopped

1 (14-ounce) container firm tofu, drained and pressed, sliced ¼-inch thick

½ teaspoon sea salt

¼ teaspoon freshly ground black pepper

2 teaspoons maple syrup

2 teaspoons red wine vinegar

Red Russian, Redbor, Lacinato, Siberian—these aren't the names of naval ships that sailed in the days of yore. They're actually varieties of one of our favorite cruciferous vegetables, kale. The truth of the matter is that we don't care *what* type you use to make this dish, because we're just happy when anyone sneaks tasty greens into their bodies before lunch.

TO PREPARE THE KALE BENEDICT

Heat a nonstick sauté pan over medium heat and add oil. Add kale and wilt slightly, 3 to 5 minutes. Add tofu to pan and sprinkle with sea salt, pepper, maple syrup, and vinegar. Cook 3 to 5 minutes. Remove kale from pan, flip tofu, and cook an additional 2 to 3 minutes. Set aside.

→

Sautéed Kale Benedict with Hollandaise Sauce *continued*

FOR THE HOLLANDAISE SAUCE

½ cup raw cashews

1 cup water

1 tablespoon freshly squeezed lemon juice, plus zest of 1 lemon

2 tablespoons vegan butter

3 tablespoons unbleached all-purpose flour

1½ cups unsweetened almond milk

½ teaspoon sea salt

¼ teaspoon cayenne pepper

¼ teaspoon ground turmeric

2 teaspoons brown rice syrup

1 teaspoon Champagne vinegar or white wine vinegar

4 to 6 thick slices fresh bread, toasted

1 tomato, cut into thin rounds

2 teaspoons fresh chives, finely chopped

TO PREPARE THE HOLLANDAISE SAUCE

1. In a high-powered blender or food processor, combine cashews, water, and lemon juice. Blend until very smooth.

2. In a medium saucepan over medium-low heat, melt butter, then add flour, and whisk to make a roux (a paste). Cook 1 minute, or until flour has a light toasted color and fragrance. Be careful not to burn. Add almond milk, sea salt, cayenne, turmeric, brown rice syrup, vinegar, and lemon zest. Whisk until smooth, then add cashew mixture. Cook for an additional 5 minutes, or until thickened. Season with more sea salt and cayenne, if desired.

3. Divide toasted bread among serving plates. Top toast with tofu and kale. Slather each piece of toast with Hollandaise sauce. Top with tomato rounds and chives. Serve warm.

TIP We stem kale by holding the base of the stem in one hand, and stripping it with the other hand, bottom to top. To clean them quickly, wash in your salad spinner like any lettuce greens.

Fresh and Spicy Bloody Mary

GLUTEN-FREE • NUT-FREE
30 MINUTES OR LESS
Serves 4 to 6
Prep time: 10 minutes
Chilling time: 20 minutes

FOR THE BLOODY MARYS

4 cups tomato-based vegetable juice

2 tablespoons freshly squeezed
  lemon juice

1 tablespoon gluten-free vegan
  Worcestershire sauce

1 to 2 teaspoons habañero hot sauce

½ teaspoon sea salt

½ teaspoon freshly ground
  black pepper

¼ teaspoon celery seed

¾ to 1 cup vodka

FOR THE TOPPINGS

6 pickle spears

1 small jar cocktail onions

6 stalks celery

8 to 10 green olives with pimentos

½ cup vegan bacon bits, for topping
  (optional)

2 tablespoons horseradish, freshly
  grated (optional)

Getting tipsy while also getting a dose of vitamin C doesn't sound half bad, does it? Not at all. Conventional Bloody Marys use non-vegan Worcestershire sauce that contains anchovies. The best vegan Worcestershire we've found is The Wizard's brand (and they even make a gluten-free version).

1. Place tomato juice in a large pitcher. Add lemon juice, Worcestershire sauce, hot sauce, sea salt, pepper, and celery seed. Blend mixture until uniform. Add vodka and stir. Chill for 20 minutes.

2. Place desired toppings on long toothpicks or skewers and add to each drink when serving. Top with bacon bits and horseradish, if desired.

TIP There are no rules when it comes to topping this veggie boozy concoction, so go wild with pickles, olives, onions, or anything else you can fit on a toothpick or straw. Bacos, the most ubiquitous form of bacon bits, just happen to be vegan.

Tropical Getaway Smoothie

GLUTEN-FREE · NUT-FREE
30 MINUTES OR LESS
Makes 1 large smoothie
Prep time: 3 minutes

1 banana, peeled and cut into chunks
¾ cup fresh or frozen diced mango
½ cup fresh or frozen diced pineapple
1 cup light coconut milk
1 tablespoon freshly squeezed
   lime juice
4 to 5 ice cubes (optional)
Toasted coconut flakes (optional)

The flavors of this smoothie will make you feel like you're drinking a piña colada with your toes in the sand. Sure, you may actually be drinking your smoothie in the car while sitting in traffic, but that doesn't mean you can't enjoy it while dreaming about your next vacation.

1. In a blender, combine banana, mango, pineapple, coconut milk, lime juice, and ice (if using fresh fruit). Blend until smooth and uniform.

2. Once blended, garnish with toasted coconut (if using).

TIP If you feel like you want to kick up your intake of greens, just throw 2 kale leaves into your smoothie. Don't worry, all the flavors of the coconut and mango will still come through.

Recipe
p.73

3

Salads

When we were kids, a fella by the name of Bob-the-Produce-Man drove up to our house with a truck that played a cute little jingle that let us know he'd arrived. When Bob opened up the back of his truck, our eyes would widen at the sight of the brilliantly colorful veggies sitting on beds of crushed ice, and tubs filled with Bob's creamy homemade ranch dressing. Bob made eating salad fun, and his magic dressing didn't hurt either. Today, we still enjoy eating fresh veggies in all forms, even without Bob's ranch. The salads in this chapter are so delicious and nutritious, we can guarantee you'll be inspired to share the love with your family and friends.

Parmesan Orzo Salad with Toasted Pecans and Cranberries

30 MINUTES OR LESS

Serves 4 to 6

Prep time: 8 minutes

Cook time: 9 minutes

FOR THE ORZO BASE

¾ teaspoon sea salt, divided

1½ cups orzo

½ teaspoon freshly ground
   black pepper

1 tablespoon brown rice syrup

2 tablespoons freshly squeezed
   lemon juice

2 tablespoons extra-virgin olive oil

FOR THE TOPPINGS

⅓ cup vegan Parmesan cheese,
   plus more if desired

¼ cup toasted pecans, coarsely
   chopped

6 to 8 fresh sage leaves, finely chopped

3 tablespoons dried cranberries

This pasta salad dish is anything but ordinary. The triple treats of vegan Parmesan, cranberries, and lemon juice meld together with the perfect balance of salty-sweet-sour. This dish tastes great either warm, at room temperature, or chilled, making it straight-up magical and the perfect picnic salad.

TO PREPARE THE ORZO BASE

1. Fill a medium saucepot about three-quarters full with water and bring to a boil. Add ¼ teaspoon sea salt. Add orzo and cook according to package directions. Drain.

2. Transfer cooked orzo into a large bowl and add remaining ½ teaspoon sea salt, pepper, brown rice syrup, lemon juice, and olive oil. Toss until well mixed.

TO ASSEMBLE THE DISH

Top orzo base with Parmesan, pecans, sage, and cranberries. Gently toss to incorporate. Season with additional sea salt and pepper, if desired, and garnish with additional Parmesan when serving, if desired.

TIP Yes, orzo looks like rice, but it's actually *pasta*. Typically, orzo dishes are served on their own, or as a side dish with soup.

Variations

For some flavor variations to the orzo salad, follow the original recipe through step 2 and use these different ingredients to assemble the dish.

Wild Mushroom and Rosemary Orzo Salad

2 teaspoons extra-virgin olive oil
2 shallots, finely chopped
6 to 8 cremini mushrooms, diced
5 to 7 oyster mushrooms, diced
2 teaspoons dry sherry
2 teaspoons red wine vinegar
2 teaspoons brown rice syrup
1 tablespoon fresh rosemary, stemmed and finely chopped

Heat a sauté pan over medium-low heat and add oil. Add shallot and cook about 2 minutes to soften. Add cremini and oyster mushrooms, sherry, vinegar, brown rice syrup, and rosemary and sauté for 5 to 7 minutes. Fold into orzo base. Serve warm or at room temperature.

Mediterranean Orzo Salad with Sun-Dried Tomatoes and Basil

1 fennel bulb, finely chopped
⅓ cup Kalamata olives, coarsely chopped
⅓ cup sun-dried tomatoes in oil, finely chopped
10 to 12 fresh basil leaves, finely chopped
2 tablespoons toasted pine nuts

Fold fennel, olives, sun-dried tomatoes, basil, and pine nuts into orzo base. Serve warm or at room temperature.

Lemon, Roasted Garbanzo, and Herb Orzo Salad

1 cup herb-roasted garbanzos (from Mixed Baby Greens and Crunchy Garbanzos, page 64)
1 tablespoon freshly squeezed lemon juice, plus zest of 1 lemon
16 to 20 fresh mint leaves, finely chopped
6 to 8 fresh basil leaves, finely chopped
¼ cup toasted pistachios, coarsely chopped

Fold in roasted chickpeas, lemon juice and zest, mint, basil, and pistachios into orzo base. Serve warm or at room temperature.

Italian Chopped Salad with Tangy Roasted Shallot Vinaigrette

GLUTEN-FREE • NUT-FREE
30 MINUTES OR LESS
Serves 4 to 6
Prep time: 10 minutes
Cook time: 20 minutes

FOR THE DRESSING

3 shallots, coarsely chopped
2 teaspoons neutral-tasting oil
3 tablespoons extra-virgin olive oil
2 tablespoons red wine vinegar
1 tablespoon Dijon mustard
3 tablespoons evaporated cane sugar
½ teaspoon gluten-free vegan
  Worcestershire sauce
¼ teaspoon garlic powder
¼ teaspoon red pepper flakes
¼ teaspoon sea salt
¼ teaspoon freshly ground
  black pepper

FOR THE SALAD

1 medium head romaine lettuce,
  finely chopped
1 avocado, peeled and chopped
1 medium tomato, chopped
3 pepperoncini, finely chopped
½ cup cooked garbanzo beans
  (chickpeas), rinsed and drained
  if canned
¼ cup chopped Persian
  (or English) cucumber
2 tablespoons oil-cured
  black olives, pitted

One of the reasons cooking is fun is because you get to use knives, so having the word "chopped" in the title just doubles the anticipated fun. This is definitely one of those salads that you can eat as a stand-alone meal since it's satisfyingly big. The flavor of the roasted shallots in the dressing ties the salad together, so you won't regret going the extra mile to roast them.

Preheat oven to 375°F.

TO PREPARE THE DRESSING

1. Place shallots and neutral-tasting oil in a small baking dish and gently turn to coat. Roast 15 to 20 minutes, or until soft and fragrant.

2. Place roasted shallots, olive oil, vinegar, mustard, sugar, Worcestershire sauce, garlic powder, red pepper flakes, sea salt, and pepper to a food processor or blender. Blend until dressing is creamy and uniform. Set aside in refrigerator until ready to use.

TO PREPARE THE SALAD

Place romaine in a large bowl with enough room to toss with dressing. Toss greens with dressing. Add avocado, tomato, pepperoncini, garbanzo beans, cucumber, and olives. Serve immediately.

TIP When chopping shallots, cut off both ends and slice them down the middle, enabling the outer skin to peel off more easily.

Baby Greens Salad with Toasted Almonds, Figs, and Champagne Vinaigrette

GLUTEN-FREE

30 MINUTES OR LESS

Serves 4 to 6

Prep time: 8 minutes

Champagne goes hand in hand with celebrations. We like to celebrate even the small things, which equates to a lot of festive drinking. It turns out that bubbly also makes killer dressing that pairs perfectly with figs.

FOR THE DRESSING

½ cup unsalted roasted almonds

5 to 8 dried unsulfured black mission figs, diced

1 cup vegan Champagne or sparkling white wine

¼ cup maple syrup

2 tablespoons neutral-tasting oil

1 teaspoon white wine vinegar

½ teaspoon sea salt

¼ teaspoon freshly ground black pepper

FOR THE SALAD

4 to 6 cups baby greens

2 Persian cucumbers (or ½ English cucumber), diced

Edible flowers, for garnish (optional)

TO PREPARE THE DRESSING

In a high-powered blender or food processor, combine almonds, figs, Champagne or sparkling white wine, maple syrup, oil, vinegar, sea salt, and pepper. Blend until smooth. Season with more sea salt and pepper, if desired. Set aside until ready to use.

TO PREPARE THE SALAD

Toss greens, cucumbers, and dressing. Top with edible flowers (if using).

TIP Not all Champagne is vegan, so check out Barnivore.com to find out if your favorite brand is animal ingredient-free. You can always sub in sparkling white wine for the Champagne, which is easier to find veganized.

Roasted Beet Caprese Salad with Toasted Walnuts

GLUTEN-FREE

Serves 4 to 6

Prep time: 10 minutes

Cook time: 1 hour 5 minutes
(or 5 minutes, if purchased
cooked beets are used)

1 to 2 red beets, whole, unpeeled

2 teaspoons neutral-tasting oil

¼ teaspoon sea salt, plus pinch,
   divided

¼ cup raw walnuts

4 ounces vegan mozzarella cheese
   or artisanal fresh vegan cheese

12 to 14 fresh basil leaves

1 tablespoon extra-virgin olive oil

1 teaspoon balsamic vinegar

¼ teaspoon freshly ground
   black pepper

TIP Artisanal vegan cheese works
well in this recipe, so spring for the
good stuff; you won't regret it!

You have choices in this life, and one of those choices is whether to cook your own beets from scratch or buy them already cooked and peeled. Both work extremely well in this Caprese salad that we "crazied-up" with beets. The addition of walnuts adds a crunchy element, tying the whole dish together.

1. Preheat oven to 375°F. Place beets in a small roasting dish. Coat in neutral-tasting oil and sprinkle with pinch sea salt. Roast for 45 minutes to 1 hour, or until a knife pierces the flesh easily and skin appears wrinkled. Remove from oven and cover with aluminum foil to steam. This helps separate skin from beet. Set aside until cool enough to peel. Reduce oven heat to 350°F.

2. Use a vegetable peeler to peel skin from beets. Slice into ¼-inch-thick rounds.

3. Place walnuts on a baking sheet and toast in oven for about 5 minutes, or until fragrant. Set aside.

4. Slice cheese into ¼-inch slices or rounds, depending on shape of cheese.

5. To assemble the salad, on a platter, place 1 slice beet, followed by 1 slice cheese, then 1 basil leaf, in rows or a round until all ingredients are used.

6. Drizzle with olive oil and vinegar, sprinkle with remaining ¼ teaspoon sea salt and pepper, and top with toasted walnuts. Serve immediately.

Vegan Cobb Salad withZesty Vinaigrette

30 MINUTES OR LESS • NUT FREE

Serves 4 to 6

Prep time: 15 minutes

Cook time: 5 minutes

Rumor has it that the Cobb salad was created in Los Angeles, the same city *we* were created in, so we have mad respect for this favorite. The traditional Cobb is far from vegan, but fear not, our version provides just as much texture and flavor.

FOR THE DRESSING

1 tablespoon vegan mayonnaise

2 tablespoons maple syrup

2 tablespoons extra-virgin olive oil

2 tablespoons red wine vinegar

1 tablespoon freshly squeezed orange juice (juice of ¼ orange)

½ teaspoon vegan Worcestershire sauce

1 teaspoon dried minced onion

¼ teaspoon garlic powder

¼ teaspoon sea salt

¼ teaspoon freshly ground black pepper

FOR THE SALAD

1 teaspoon vegan butter

4 or 5 strips tempeh bacon, diced

1 large head romaine lettuce, finely chopped

1 small tomato, chopped

½ avocado, peeled and chopped

¼ cup shredded carrot

¼ cup Persian (or English) cucumber, finely diced

⅓ cup savory baked tofu, diced

¼ cup shredded vegan cheese

TO PREPARE THE DRESSING

Place mayonnaise, maple syrup, oil, vinegar, orange juice, Worcestershire sauce, onion, garlic powder, sea salt, and pepper in a food processor or blender. Blend until creamy and uniform. Set aside until ready to assemble salad.

TO PREPARE THE SALAD

1. Heat a small sauté pan over medium heat and add butter. Add tempeh bacon and cook 3 to 5 minutes, or until browned. Set aside.

2. Toss romaine with desired amount of dressing and divide among plates. Place tomato, avocado, carrot, cucumber, tofu, tempeh bacon, and cheese in bunches over tossed salad greens.

Greek Salad with Tofu Feta

30 MINUTES OR LESS
GLUTEN FREE
Serves 4 to 6
Prep time: 25 minutes

FOR THE TOFU FETA

1 (14-ounce) container firm tofu, drained, pressed, and cut into small cubes

2 teaspoons light miso paste

½ teaspoon sea salt

½ teaspoon dried basil

½ teaspoon dried oregano

¼ cup freshly squeezed lemon juice

¼ cup extra-virgin olive oil

FOR THE DRESSING

2 tablespoons extra-virgin olive oil

1 tablespoon agave

1 tablespoon freshly squeezed lemon juice

1 teaspoon red wine vinegar

¼ teaspoon sea salt

¼ teaspoon freshly ground black pepper

FOR THE SALAD

2 to 3 Persian (or 1 English) cucumbers, cut in half lengthwise, then sliced

1 cup cherry tomatoes, halved

¼ cup Kalamata olives, sliced

½ red or orange bell pepper, diced

¼ red onion, thinly sliced (or diced, if preferred)

2 tablespoons pine nuts (optional)

We spent a month traveling around Greece, relaxing on the beaches, climbing around historic ruins, staying out late dancing, and making new friends. But to be honest, most of our time was spent eating Greek food, especially the famous Greek salad (ordered with no cheese!). We got home and decided we had to recreate it so we wouldn't have to wait until our next trip to the Mediterranean.

TO PREPARE THE FETA

Place tofu in a bowl and coat with miso, sea salt, basil, oregano, lemon juice, and oil. Set aside for about 10 minutes to develop flavors.

TO PREPARE THE DRESSING

Whisk oil, agave, lemon juice, vinegar, sea salt, and pepper in a small bowl. Set aside.

TO ASSEMBLE THE SALAD

In a large bowl, toss cucumbers, tomatoes, olives, bell pepper, and onion with dressing. Gently fold in feta when ready to serve. Sprinkle with pine nuts (if using).

TIP The tofu feta can be used in many recipes, not just this salad. Throw it over couscous, add it to pasta, or sub it into recipes that call for dairy-based feta.

Refreshing Green Salad with Creamy Papaya Dressing

GLUTEN-FREE

30 MINUTES OR LESS

Serves 4 to 6

Prep time: 10 minutes

FOR THE DRESSING

1 tablespoon papaya seeds

½ large papaya,
   seeded and peeled

2 tablespoons neutral-tasting oil

¼ cup brown rice syrup

1 tablespoon maple syrup

3 tablespoons freshly squeezed
   lime juice

1 tablespoon rice vinegar

¼ teaspoon sea salt

¼ teaspoon freshly ground
   black pepper

FOR THE SALAD

1 large head romaine lettuce,
   chopped

1 avocado, peeled and diced

½ cup shredded carrot

¼ red onion, thinly sliced

¼ cup macadamia nuts,
   coarsely chopped

Aloha! This salad was inspired by our favorite island state. Back in the day, some genius figured out that you can eat papaya seeds in place of black pepper. These nutrient-packed seeds have been consumed for thousands of years. They're an anti-inflammatory, and contain potent enzymes that aid both in digestion and detoxification. Seeds aside, papayas are already chock-full of good-for-you vitamins, minerals, and antioxidants. So what are you waiting for? Go out and buy one. Now!

FOR THE DRESSING

Place papaya seeds in a food processor or blender. Add papaya flesh, oil, brown rice syrup, maple syrup, lime juice, vinegar, sea salt, and pepper. Blend until dressing is creamy and uniform.

FOR THE SALAD

In a large bowl, toss romaine with desired amount of dressing. Top with avocado, carrot, onion, and macadamia nuts.

TIP The seeds aren't the only good-for-you parts of papayas. These tasty fruits are packed with healthy minerals like copper, potassium, and magnesium while also containing vitamins like B and C. This combo of nutrients is really healthy for the cardio-vascular system.

Mixed Baby Greens and Crunchy Garbanzos with Roasted Red Pepper Dressing

GLUTEN-FREE • NUT-FREE
30 MINUTES OR LESS
Serves 4 to 6
Prep time: 12 minutes
Cook time: 14 minutes

If you look at a garbanzo bean for more than two seconds, you'll notice it resembles a tiny ram's head. Actually, the name "garbanzo" translated from Latin means "small ram." The crunchy garbanzos coupled with the creamy and zingy roasted red pepper dressing give this salad a unique Italian flair.

Preheat oven to 375°F.

FOR THE DRESSING

1 roasted red bell pepper, coarsely chopped

¼ cup extra-virgin olive oil

2 teaspoons agave or brown rice syrup

1 tablespoon freshly squeezed lemon juice

1 teaspoon Dijon mustard

¼ teaspoon sea salt

¼ teaspoon freshly ground black pepper

TO PREPARE THE DRESSING

Place bell pepper in food processor or blender. Add oil, agave or brown rice syrup, lemon juice, mustard, sea salt, and pepper. Blend until creamy and uniform.

FOR THE BEANS

1 (15-ounce) can garbanzo beans (chickpeas), rinsed and drained

1 tablespoon freshly squeezed lemon juice

1 tablespoon neutral-tasting oil

½ teaspoon dried thyme

½ teaspoon sea salt

¼ teaspoon freshly ground black pepper

4 cups packed baby lettuce or mixed lettuce greens

1 medium tomato, chopped

1 Persian (or ½ English) cucumber, cut into rounds

¼ cup shredded carrot

TO PREPARE THE BEANS

Add garbanzo beans to a medium bowl. Toss with lemon juice, oil, thyme, sea salt, and pepper. Place in a small baking dish and roast about 12 to 14 minutes, shaking pan occasionally.

TO ASSEMBLE THE SALAD

In a large bowl, toss greens with desired amount of dressing and top with garbanzos, tomato, cucumber, and carrot.

TIP If you roast your own bell peppers, here's an easy way to get them out of their skins: Cover roasted bell peppers with foil once they come out of the oven. Let them sit and steam for about 20 minutes before peeling. This will separate the skin from the flesh.

Mexican Street Corn and Black Bean Salad over Greens

GLUTEN-FREE • **NUT-FREE**
30 MINUTES OR LESS

Serves 4 to 6
Prep time: 10 minutes
Cook time: 11 minutes

If you've ever witnessed Mexican street corn being prepared, you know the recipe doesn't skimp on mayo and cheese. This is a lightened up, "salady" version of the Mexican street food staple that has all the creamy richness of the original, plus vegan twists that make it pop.

2 teaspoons vegan butter

2 cloves garlic, finely chopped

½ red onion, finely chopped

2 or 3 ears of corn (or 2 cups frozen corn kernels, thawed)

1 (15-ounce) can black beans, rinsed and drained

¼ cup vegan mayonnaise

¼ teaspoon chipotle powder

¼ teaspoon sea salt

¼ teaspoon freshly ground black pepper

1 tablespoon freshly squeezed lemon juice, plus zest of ½ lemon

2 teaspoons maple syrup

1 to 2 cups baby kale or romaine lettuce, chopped

2 tablespoons fresh cilantro, coarsely chopped, for garnish

¼ block vegan Jack or mozzarella cheese, crumbled, for garnish

1 tablespoon vegan Parmesan, for garnish

1. Heat a medium sauté pan over medium heat and add butter. Add garlic and onion and cook 2 to 3 minutes to soften slightly. Add corn and cook 5 to 6 minutes, or until golden and slightly charred. Add beans and cook 2 additional minutes. Remove from heat.

2. Transfer bean and corn mixture to a large bowl and set aside.

3. In a separate bowl, combine mayonnaise, chipotle, sea salt, pepper, lemon juice and zest, and maple syrup. Whisk until uniform and add to corn and bean mixture. Fold to incorporate.

4. Place kale or romaine in a shallow dish and top with bean and corn mixture. Garnish with cilantro, Jack or mozzarella cheese, and Parmesan. Serve warm or at room temperature.

TIP If fresh corn isn't in season, we recommend using frozen corn. If that's not available, purchase canned corn. There you have it, in order of our preference!

Smoky Shiitake Bacon Wedge Salad

Serves 4

Prep time: 15 minutes,
plus 10 minutes to marinate

Cook time: 20 minutes

FOR THE SHIITAKE BACON

1 tablespoon neutral-tasting oil

1 tablespoon maple syrup

2 teaspoons sherry vinegar

½ teaspoon liquid smoke

¼ teaspoon smoked sea salt

¼ teaspoon freshly ground
   black pepper

10 to 15 shiitake mushrooms,
   stemmed and cut into thin strips

FOR THE DRESSING

½ cup vegan mayonnaise

¼ cup vegan sour cream

2 tablespoons unsweetened
   almond milk

1 teaspoon maple syrup

1 teaspoon vegan
   Worcestershire sauce

2 teaspoons Dijon or stone-ground
   mustard

2 teaspoons freshly squeezed
   lemon juice and zest of ½ lemon

¼ teaspoon sea salt

¼ teaspoon freshly ground
   black pepper

¼ teaspoon garlic powder

6 ounces vegan blue cheese or
   vegan ricotta

1 head iceberg lettuce, quartered

This is the Frank Sinatra of salads: popular, timeless, and bold. The crisp wedges of iceberg lettuce form the perfect stage for the real stars of the show, smoky shiitake bacon and thick blue cheese dressing.

Preheat oven to 400°F.

TO PREPARE THE SHIITAKE BACON

In a bowl combine oil, maple syrup, vinegar, liquid smoke, smoked sea salt, and pepper. Whisk. Add mushrooms and marinate for about 10 minutes. Place mushrooms on baking sheet lined with a silicone mat or greased parchment paper. Bake for 15 to 20 minutes, flipping once.

TO PREPARE THE DRESSING

In a medium bowl, combine mayonnaise, sour cream, almond milk, maple syrup, Worcestershire sauce, mustard, lemon juice, sea salt, pepper, and garlic powder. Whisk to incorporate. Crumble in blue or ricotta cheese. Whisk to combine.

Place lettuce wedges on salad plates. Drizzle each generously with dressing and top with a few pieces of bacon per plate.

TIP The easiest way to prepare your iceberg lettuce is to trim out the core, run the lettuce upside down under cold water, and then place right-side up over a colander, to drain and dry.

Asian Cucumber and Sea Vegetable Salad

GLUTEN-FREE • NUT-FREE
30 MINUTES OR LESS
Serves 4 to 6
Prep time: 10 minutes

FOR THE DRESSING

3 tablespoons brown rice vinegar

2 tablespoons freshly squeezed
  lemon juice, plus zest of 1 lemon

1 tablespoon toasted sesame oil

1 tablespoon evaporated cane sugar

1 tablespoon pickled ginger,
  finely chopped

1 teaspoon dried minced onion

½ teaspoon sea salt

2 teaspoons sesame seeds,
  plus more for garnish

FOR THE SALAD

¼ cup dried wakame seaweed

2 hothouse cucumbers,
  cut into ¼-inch-thick rounds

½ cup shredded carrots

Who would have guessed that cucumbers and seaweed could be such good friends? One grows up high on the vine, while the other is born on the mean streets of the ocean floor. This salad is refreshing: crunchy and light with a subtle, tangy punch. It makes the perfect side dish complement to heavier fare.

TO PREPARE THE DRESSING

In a bowl, whisk vinegar, lemon juice and zest, oil, sugar, ginger, dried onion, sea salt, and 2 teaspoons sesame seeds.

TO PREPARE THE SALAD

1. Soak wakame in warm water for 3 to 5 minutes to rehydrate. Drain, and chop if desired. Place in large serving bowl. Add cucumbers and carrot to bowl with wakame.

2. Add dressing to salad and toss. Serve right away, garnished with additional sesame seeds.

TIP If you have a food processor, use the slicing blade attachment for cucumbers and the shredding attachment for carrots to make this preparation go lightning fast.

TIP Replace the wakame with scallions if sea veggies aren't your thing.

Chinese Un-Chicken Salad with Crunchies

30 MINUTES OR LESS

Serves 4 to 6

Prep time: 10 minutes

Cook time: 8 minutes

FOR THE DRESSING

2 tablespoons agave

2 tablespoons freshly squeezed
   lime juice, plus zest of 1 lime

1 tablespoon neutral-tasting oil

1 tablespoon rice vinegar

1 teaspoon hot chili sesame oil

2 tablespoons pickled ginger,
   finely chopped

1 tablespoon sesame seeds

½ teaspoon sea salt

¼ teaspoon freshly ground
   black pepper

FOR THE SALAD

¼ cup neutral-tasting oil, plus
   2 teaspoons, divided

¼ cup vermicelli rice noodles,
   broken into 1-inch pieces

1 tablespoon brown rice vinegar

2 teaspoons tamari

1 teaspoon hot chili sesame oil

2 teaspoons agave

¼ teaspoon freshly ground
   black pepper

2 cups vegan chicken, diced

6 cups romaine lettuce, chopped

¼ cup slivered almonds

2 teaspoons sesame seeds (optional)

Hold the chicken, and add your favorite vegan substitute to this amazing salad. It has snap, zing, pow . . . and sesame seeds. What more could you want? The dressing can also double as a marinade for tofu, tempeh, or seitan, making your stir-fry dishes even quicker to put together.

TO PREPARE THE DRESSING

In a small bowl, whisk together agave, lime juice and zest, neutral-tasting oil, vinegar, sesame oil, ginger, sesame seeds, sea salt, and pepper. Set aside.

TO PREPARE THE SALAD

1. In a medium pot over medium heat, heat ¼ cup oil until ripples appear. Add small amount of noodles. Noodles will crisp and expand fast, so after about 5 seconds remove with a slotted spoon and place on a paper towel-lined plate to drain. Repeat for all noodles and set aside.

2. For the chicken marinade, in a small bowl, whisk vinegar, tamari, remaining 2 teaspoons neutral-tasting oil, sesame oil, agave, and pepper. Heat a small skillet over medium heat, and add chicken and marinade. Cook for 3 to 5 minutes, or until slightly charred.

3. In a large bowl, toss greens with dressing and sprinkle with the crunchy noodles and almonds. Place chicken on top and sprinkle with sesame seeds (if using).

TIP Store all sesame products in the refrigerator, including seeds and oil. They go rancid quickly and this will help preserve them.

TIP If you prefer less crunch, replace the crunchies with fresh bean sprouts.

Spiced Moroccan Carrot Salad

GLUTEN-FREE

Serves 4 to 6

Prep time: 10 minutes,
plus 30 minutes to marinate

3 or 4 large carrots

½ teaspoon ground cumin

¼ teaspoon cayenne pepper

¼ teaspoon ground coriander

2 tablespoons freshly squeezed
lemon juice, plus zest of ½ lemon

1 teaspoon Champagne or
red wine vinegar

1 teaspoon maple syrup

¼ teaspoon orange flower water

1 small clove garlic, finely chopped

10 to 12 fresh mint leaves, finely
chopped, plus more for garnish

1 tablespoon toasted pistachios,
chopped, for garnish

When you purchase a big bag of carrots, you have basically three choices: juice 'em, soup 'em, or salad 'em. Our Spiced Moroccan Carrot Salad will creatively repurpose your crunchy root veggies. If you purchase heirloom carrots, this salad comes to life with beautiful colors, flavors, and a variety of antioxidants.

1. In a food processor fitted with a shredding attachment, shred carrots and place in a large bowl. Or you can use a hand grater with large holes.

2. Add cumin, cayenne, coriander, lemon juice and zest, vinegar, maple syrup, orange flower water, garlic, and mint. Garnish with pistachios and additional mint. Marinate in refrigerator for 30 minutes for optimal flavor. Serve chilled.

TIP Orange flower water is a powerful extract of distilled orange blossoms. It's used in sweet and savory Moroccan and North African dishes for aroma and to add a unique flavor.

Bayou Coleslaw

GLUTEN-FREE • NUT-FREE

Serves 4 to 6

Prep time: 15 minutes,
plus 10 minutes to marinate

Cook time: 35 minutes

FOR THE DRESSING

1 bulb garlic, top sliced off to
  expose cloves

¼ teaspoon neutral-tasting oil

½ teaspoon sea salt, plus pinch,
  divided

½ teaspoon freshly ground
  black pepper, plus pinch,
  divided

1 cup vegan mayonnaise

3 tablespoons freshly squeezed
  lemon juice, plus zest of ½ lemon

2 tablespoons brown rice syrup

2 teaspoons hot sauce

2 teaspoons fresh scallions,
  finely chopped

1 heaping teaspoon Cajun seasoning

1 teaspoon dried minced onion

½ teaspoon celery seeds

FOR THE RAISINS

¼ cup raisins or currants

1 tablespoon freshly squeezed
  lemon juice

1 tablespoon maple syrup

Dash bourbon (optional)

FOR THE SALAD

½ head green cabbage, shredded

¼ head red cabbage, shredded

1 carrot, thinly sliced

"Son of a gun, we'll have big fun on the bayou"—
because we will be eating this coleslaw. We
think Hank Williams would have approved of the
flavors we threw into this Louisiana special, which
contains a touch of hot sauce, currants for sweetness, and a rich blend of Southern seasonings.

Preheat oven to 375°F.

TO PREPARE THE DRESSING

1.   Place garlic bulb cut-side down in a heatproof
ramekin. Drizzle with oil. Sprinkle with pinch sea salt
and pepper. Roast for 35 minutes, or until cloves are soft.

2.   When cool enough to handle, remove 3 to 5 cloves
roasted garlic from the bulb and use the blade of a knife
to squeeze flesh out of skin into a mixing bowl, then
smooth it to a paste. Add mayonnaise, lemon juice
and zest, brown rice syrup, hot sauce, scallions, Cajun
seasoning, minced onion, celery seeds, and remaining
½ teaspoon sea salt and ½ teaspoon pepper. Whisk
until uniform.

TO PREPARE THE RAISINS

Place the raisins (or currants, if preferred) in a small
bowl and add lemon juice, maple syrup, and bourbon
(if using). Set aside to marinate about 10 minutes.

TO ASSEMBLE THE SALAD

In a large serving bowl, combine cabbages and carrot.
Add dressing and mix until well coated. Top with
marinated raisins or currants.

TIP Cutting the cabbage and letting it rest for 10 minutes
before dressing it can help release the cancer-fighting sulfur
compounds in this bad boy.

Bibb Lettuce and Radish Salad with Chive Buttermilk Dressing

GLUTEN-FREE • NUT-FREE

Serves 4 to 6

Prep time: 5 minutes

Cook time: 35 minutes

1 bulb garlic, top sliced off to expose cloves

¼ teaspoon neutral-tasting oil

¼ teaspoon sea salt, plus pinch, divided

¼ teaspoon freshly ground black pepper, plus pinch, divided

⅓ cup soy milk creamer

1 teaspoon apple cider vinegar

¼ cup vegan mayonnaise

2 teaspoons freshly squeezed lemon juice

2 teaspoons maple syrup

2 tablespoons fresh chives, coarsely chopped

1 head Bibb lettuce, roughly chopped

4 to 6 radishes, cut into thin strips

1 avocado, peeled and cut into thin segments

At first glance this salad seems simple, but don't let her fool ya. She gets her delicate nature from the Bibb lettuce, spicy demeanor from the radishes, and a li'l spunk from the buttermilk dressing, made by curdling soy milk creamer with vinegar. This salad has a ton of personality.

1. Preheat oven to 375°F. Place garlic cut-side down in heatproof ramekin. Drizzle with oil. Sprinkle with pinch sea salt and pepper. Roast for 35 minutes, or until cloves are soft.

2. Combine creamer and vinegar in a bowl. Whisk gently and set aside for 1 to 2 minutes.

3. When cool enough to handle, remove 3 or 4 cloves roasted garlic from the bulb and use the blade of a knife to squeeze flesh out of skin into a blender or food processor. Add curdled creamer, mayonnaise, lemon juice, maple syrup, and remaining ¼ teaspoon sea salt and ¼ teaspoon pepper. Blend until smooth and fold in chives.

4. To serve salad, divide lettuce among salad plates. Drizzle with dressing. Top each serving with radishes and avocado.

TIP When storing radishes in the refrigerator, don't wash them; they will go bad more quickly. Be sure to remove the leaves, however, as they leach moisture from the radishes, drying them out prematurely.

Recipe
p.86

Soups & Stews

There is a beautiful simplicity in creating soups and stews, as they take us back to an earlier time. We mean *way* back. Humans have been eating soups and stews for thousands of years. Imagine this: You forage all day for sustenance, you toss your bounty into a giant clay pot, and you cook it slowly over an open fire in order to create a meal that feeds and comforts your entire family.

Fast-forward to modern times and we still find the same comfort in making soups and stews in our homes. In this chapter we've assembled a variety of recipes from across the globe that will surely keep the whole village smiling.

Velvety Kale Soup
with Cashew Cream

GLUTEN-FREE

Serves 4 to 6

Prep time: 18 minutes

Cook time: 1 hour

FOR THE SOUP

1 bulb garlic, top sliced off to
  expose the cloves

¼ teaspoon neutral-tasting oil

¾ teaspoon sea salt, plus pinch,
  divided

½ teaspoon freshly ground
  black pepper, plus pinch,
  divided

2 tablespoons vegan butter

1 medium yellow onion, finely chopped

1 large potato, peeled and diced
  (about ¾ cup)

1 bay leaf

1 large bunch kale, stemmed and
  chopped (about 3 loose cups)

1 bunch spinach, coarsely chopped
  (about 3 loose cups)

2½ cups reduced-sodium
  vegetable broth

¼ cup Marsala wine

1 cup soy milk creamer

The Fountain of Youth isn't really a fountain, it's a bowl of kale soup. Fully loaded with greens and drizzled with cashew cream, this warming, nutrient-rich dish is packed with antioxidants and fiber—it's basically nature's Botox.

Preheat oven to 375°F.

TO PREPARE THE SOUP

1. Place garlic bulb cut-side down in a heatproof ramekin. Drizzle with oil and sprinkle with pinch sea salt and pepper. Roast for 35 minutes, or until cloves are soft.

2. Heat a large stockpot over medium heat. Add butter and onion. Remove 4 or 5 cloves roasted garlic from the bulb and use the blade of a knife to squeeze flesh out of skin into the pot. Cook for 3 to 5 minutes, or until slightly softened. Add potato, bay leaf, and remaining ¾ teaspoon sea salt and ½ teaspoon pepper. Cook for an additional 2 to 3 minutes.

3. Add kale and spinach and sauté for about 3 more minutes to wilt.

4. Add broth, wine, and creamer. Reduce heat to a simmer and cook, partially covered, for about 18 minutes, or until potatoes are very tender. Discard bay leaf.

5. Using an immersion blender, purée soup. Alternately, blend soup mixture in a blender, with middle of lid removed, covered in a clean kitchen towel. Only fill blender halfway at a time, to prevent spillage. Season with more sea salt and pepper, if desired.

FOR THE CASHEW CREAM

⅓ cup unsalted raw cashews

1 teaspoon freshly squeezed lemon juice

¼ cup soy milk creamer or almond milk

Pinch garlic powder

Pinch sea salt

Pinch freshly ground black pepper

TO MAKE THE CASHEW CREAM

In a high-powered blender or food processor, combine cashews, lemon juice, creamer or almond milk, garlic powder, sea salt, and pepper and blend until smooth.

Ladle soup into bowls and drizzle each portion with cashew cream.

TIP Even though your greens will shrink by about 90 percent when you cook this soup, you'll still need a lot of room, so be sure to use a large pot.

Creamy Carrot Soup with Cashew Cream and Fresh Dill

6 large carrots, coarsely chopped

3 tablespoons vegan white wine

4 cups reduced-sodium vegetable broth

2 tablespoons fresh dill, coarsely chopped

1. Follow steps 1 and 2 as written in original recipe.

2. In step 3, substitute carrots for greens.

3. In step 4, substitute white wine for Marsala and add increased quantity of broth (4 cups).

4. Follow step 5 as written in original recipe.

5. Garnish with dill immediately before serving.

Cream of Cauliflower Soup with Fresh Chives

1 stalk celery, finely chopped

1 carrot, finely chopped

1 head cauliflower, coarsely chopped

1 tablespoon nutritional yeast

2 cups reduced-sodium vegetable broth

2 cups unsweetened almond or soy milk

1 tablespoon freshly squeezed lemon juice, plus zest of 1 lemon

2 tablespoons fresh chives, finely chopped

1. Follow step 1 as written in original recipe.

2. In step 2, add celery and carrot.

3. In step 3, substitute cauliflower and nutritional yeast for greens.

4. In step 4, substitute broth and almond or soy milk for wine, broth, and creamer.

5. Follow step 5 as written in original recipe.

6. To serve, add lemon juice and zest, and garnish with chives.

Creamy Butternut Squash and Apple Soup with Cashew Cream

3 small carrots, diced

2 stalks celery, diced

1 Granny Smith apple, peeled, cored, and diced

1 small butternut squash, peeled, seeded, and diced

2 teaspoons fresh rosemary, stemmed and finely chopped

½ teaspoon sea salt

½ teaspoon freshly ground black pepper

⅛ teaspoon freshly grated nutmeg

4 cups reduced-sodium vegetable broth

1. Follow steps 1 and 2 as written in original recipe.

2. In steps 3 and 4, substitute carrots, celery, and apple for greens, and cook for about 7 minutes. Add squash, rosemary, sea salt, pepper, nutmeg, and broth. Cook for 15 to 18 minutes, or until butternut squash is tender.

3. Follow step 5 as written in original recipe.

Classic Minestrone Soup

NUT-FREE

Serves 4 to 6

Prep time: 10 minutes

Cook time: 25 minutes

1 tablespoon extra-virgin olive oil

1 medium yellow onion, finely chopped

2 cloves garlic, finely chopped

1 carrot, diced

1 potato, peeled and diced

1 zucchini, diced

1 bay leaf

¼ teaspoon dried basil

¼ teaspoon dried oregano

½ teaspoon sea salt

½ teaspoon freshly ground
   black pepper

1 (14.5-ounce) can diced
   tomatoes, undrained

6 cups reduced-sodium
   vegetable broth

1 cup mini pasta shells or star pasta

1 tablespoon freshly squeezed
   lemon juice

2 teaspoons brown rice syrup

Minestrone is the soup loved by everyone, from finicky eaters to the most discerning gourmets. After all, what's not to love? The unbeatable combo of fresh veggies, Italian herbs, and tiny pasta gives this soup its distinctive crowd-pleasing complexity.

1. Heat a 6-quart saucepan over medium-low heat. Add oil, onion, and garlic and sauté about 3 minutes, or just until soft. Add carrot, potato, and zucchini and sauté for 3 to 4 additional minutes. Add bay leaf, basil, oregano, sea salt, and pepper.

2. Add tomatoes and broth, and bring soup to a simmer. Add pasta. Cover pan with a lid and cook for 15 to 18 minutes, or until noodles are cooked through. Discard bay leaf.

3. When noodles are soft, add lemon juice and brown rice syrup and stir to incorporate. Season soup with more sea salt and pepper, if desired.

TIP   To make this soup gluten-free, just switch out your wheat pasta to a gluten-free variety, such as brown rice mini-shells. The cooking time will vary slightly, based on the brand and type of pasta you use.

Blue Ribbon Chili with Sour Cream and Chives

NUT-FREE

Serves 4 to 6

Prep time: 15 minutes

Cook time: 30 minutes

2 teaspoons neutral-tasting oil

½ yellow onion, finely chopped

2 cloves garlic, minced

2 zucchini, diced

1 (8-ounce) package seitan, crumbled or finely chopped

½ teaspoon ground cumin

½ teaspoon smoked paprika

½ teaspoon sea salt

1 tablespoon brown sugar

1 cinnamon stick

1 (28-ounce) can diced tomatoes, undrained

1 tablespoon molasses

2 teaspoons unsweetened cocoa powder

⅔ cup reduced-sodium vegetable broth

1 (15-ounce) can red kidney beans, rinsed and drained

1 (15-ounce) can white beans, rinsed and drained

1 tablespoon freshly squeezed lemon juice

¼ cup vegan sour cream

2 tablespoons fresh chives, finely chopped

This one-pot wonder has been a hit in our cooking classes for years. We all have some cans of beans in the cupboard, some fresh veggies in the drawer, and a little carton of veggie broth hiding in the back of the pantry. These simple ingredients bring this dish to life, even when the fridge looks empty.

1. Heat oil in a large saucepan over medium-low heat. Add onion, garlic, zucchini, and seitan. Sauté for 3 to 5 minutes, or until onions are soft.

2. Add cumin, paprika, sea salt, brown sugar, and cinnamon stick. Sauté for 1 additional minute.

3. Add tomatoes, molasses, cocoa powder, broth, kidney beans, white beans, and lemon juice. Cook, covered, on medium-low heat for 15 to 20 minutes, stirring occasionally. Remove lid and cook an additional 5 to 8 minutes to thicken up chili. Remove cinnamon stick before serving.

4. Ladle warm chili into bowls. Top with sour cream and chives.

TIP Chili freezes well, so make a big ol' batch for those days when you need to come home from work, get into pajamas early, and enjoy an effortless meal.

Sesame Miso Soup with Ginger and Tofu

GLUTEN-FREE • NUT-FREE
30 MINUTES OR LESS
Serves 4 to 6
Prep time: 8 minutes
Cook time: 13 minutes

2 teaspoons neutral-tasting oil

6 ounces firm silken tofu

4 to 6 shiitake mushrooms, stemmed and cut into thin strips

1 small carrot, grated (about ¼ cup)

5 cups reduced-sodium vegetable broth

⅓ cup light miso paste

2 teaspoons toasted sesame oil, plus dash for serving

2 teaspoons tamari

2 teaspoons fresh ginger, finely grated

4 scallions, finely chopped, for garnish

1 teaspoon sesame seeds, for garnish

Need a bowl of soup in a hurry? Make miso soup! Want to consume more probiotics? Make miso soup! Feel a cold coming on? Make miso soup! It's so much more than an afterthought included with your bento box lunch. Our version is loaded with shiitake mushrooms, a hint of sesame oil, and lots of veggies.

1. Heat a 4-quart saucepan over medium heat. Add neutral-tasting oil, tofu, mushrooms, and carrot and cook for 2 to 3 minutes. Add broth and bring to a simmer.

2. Decrease heat to medium-low and add miso. Whisk until miso is dissolved. Add sesame oil, tamari, and ginger and cook 7 to 10 minutes to allow flavors to develop.

3. Serve warm, garnished with scallions, dash sesame oil, and sesame seeds.

TIP To preserve the probiotics in miso paste, warm up the soup slowly to avoid boiling the broth.

Tortilla Soup with Ancho Cream Topping

GLUTEN-FREE · NUT-FREE

Serves 4 to 6

Prep time: 10 minutes

Cook time: 25 minutes

FOR THE SOUP

1 tablespoon neutral-tasting oil

1 medium yellow onion, finely chopped

1 clove garlic, finely chopped

½ red bell pepper, finely chopped

1 small carrot, diced

3 (9-inch) gluten-free corn tortillas, roughly chopped

½ teaspoon sea salt

¼ teaspoon freshly ground black pepper

½ teaspoon ground cumin

¼ teaspoon chipotle powder

1 bay leaf

1 (28-ounce) can diced tomatoes, undrained

4 cups reduced-sodium vegetable broth

1 tablespoon agave

1 tablespoon freshly squeezed lime juice

2 teaspoons fresh oregano, finely chopped

Tortillas are so versatile—they envelop your burrito one minute, make crunchy dipping chips the next, and even thicken a soup like nobody's business. This smooth but hearty soup has a touch of heat and tanginess enhanced by the toasty flavor of tortillas. You'll spend less time making this soup than you would on a run to your local taqueria!

TO PREPARE THE SOUP

1. Heat a 6-quart saucepan over medium heat. Add oil and sauté onion, garlic, bell pepper, and carrot for 3 to 5 minutes, or until soft. Add tortillas and cook for 2 additional minutes. Add sea salt, pepper, cumin, chipotle, and bay leaf and cook for about 2 more minutes.

2. Add tomatoes, broth, agave, lime juice, and oregano. Reduce heat to medium and simmer, partially covered, for 12 to 15 minutes, or until tortillas are soft. Discard bay leaf.

3. Using an immersion blender, blend soup mixture until smooth. Alternatively, process in batches using a traditional blender, being careful to place a towel over the hole in the blender lid so that steam will be able to escape.

FOR THE ANCHO CREAM

1 cup vegan sour cream

2 teaspoons agave

2 teaspoons freshly squeezed
   lemon juice

½ teaspoon ancho chile powder

¼ teaspoon garlic powder

¼ teaspoon sea salt

FOR THE ANCHO CREAM

In a mixing bowl, combine sour cream, agave, lemon juice, ancho chile powder, garlic powder, and sea salt. Whisk until smooth.

Season soup with more sea salt and pepper, if desired, and serve warm in bowls, topped with ancho cream.

TIP If you have ancho cream left over, use it as a dip for tortilla chips.

Chicken Noodle Soup

NUT-FREE

Serves 4 to 6

Prep time: 10 minutes

Cook time: 25 minutes

1 tablespoon vegan butter

1 medium yellow onion, finely chopped

2 cloves garlic, finely chopped

1 carrot, diced

2 stalks celery, diced

2 cups vegan chicken, diced

1 teaspoon poultry seasoning
  spice blend

½ teaspoon sea salt

½ teaspoon freshly ground
  black pepper

1 bay leaf

6 cups reduced-sodium
  vegetable broth

1 cup water

1½ cups spaghetti, broken into
  2-inch pieces

1 tablespoon freshly squeezed
  lemon juice

1 teaspoon brown rice syrup

2 tablespoons fresh flat-leaf parsley,
  coarsely chopped (optional)

This soup is the king of all comfort foods for good reason. It earned its crown by crossing continents, providing warmth and nourishment to cultures worldwide. There are a ton of different textures in this soup, so we leave it to you to decide whether to use a fork, spoon, or spork, or sip it straight from the bowl when no one's looking.

1. Heat a 4-quart saucepan over medium heat. Add butter, onion, and garlic. Cook 3 to 5 minutes, or until softened.

2. Add carrot, celery, chicken, poultry seasoning, sea salt, pepper, and bay leaf. Cook 3 to 4 additional minutes.

3. Add broth, water, and spaghetti pieces, cover pan with a lid, and bring soup to a simmer. Cook 16 to 18 minutes, or until noodles are cooked through. Discard bay leaf.

4. Remove from heat and add lemon juice and brown rice syrup. Add more sea salt and pepper, if desired.

5. Top with parsley (if using) and serve warm.

TIP For a gluten-free version that even Grandma would love, use rice noodles and gluten-free vegan chicken.

Lemongrass-Scented Coconut Tofu Soup

GLUTEN-FREE • NUT-FREE

Serves 4 to 6

Prep time: 10 minutes

Cook time: 25 minutes, plus 30 minutes to rest

2 teaspoons virgin coconut oil

5 shiitake mushrooms, stemmed and cut into large slices

½ block extra-firm tofu (6 ounces), drained, pressed, and diced

1 (2-inch) piece galangal root, peeled and sliced

4 to 6 whole kaffir lime leaves

1 large stalk lemongrass, sliced into 1-inch rounds

2 teaspoons fresh ginger, grated

¼ teaspoon red pepper flakes (optional)

2 (13.5-ounce) cans full-fat coconut milk

1 cup reduced-sodium vegetable broth

¾ teaspoon sea salt

2 teaspoons brown rice syrup or agave

3 tablespoons freshly squeezed lime juice, plus more for serving

You may not be familiar with fresh lemongrass, galangal, and kaffir lime leaves, but fear not! This Thai-inspired soup is the belle of the bowl and worth a quick trip to your local Asian market because these authentic ingredients make this satisfying soup a standout.

1. Heat a 6-quart saucepan over medium heat. Add oil, mushrooms, and tofu. Sauté until golden brown, 3 to 5 minutes. Add galangal, kaffir lime leaves, lemongrass, ginger, and red pepper flakes (if using). Add coconut milk, broth, sea salt, brown rice syrup or agave, and lime juice. Whisk.

2. Reduce heat to medium-low, cover the pan with a lid, and simmer for 15 to 20 minutes.

3. Remove from heat and let sit for about 30 minutes to let flavors develop. Reheat over low heat. Remove the galangal, kaffir lime leaves, and lemongrass and serve warm, with a squeeze of additional lime juice.

TIP Lemongrass, galangal, and kaffir lime leaves provide a depth of flavor in the soup broth, but shouldn't be eaten.

French Pistou Soup

Serves 4 to 6
Prep time: 15 minutes
Cook time: 30 minutes

Think of this soup as a French take on minestrone, with a punch of pure pesto stirred in. Serve it with a baguette and a glass of *vin* and transport yourself to Provence and those lovely lavender fields.

FOR THE SOUP

1 tablespoon extra-virgin olive oil

1 medium yellow onion, finely chopped

2 cloves garlic, finely chopped

2 small zucchini, diced

1 small carrot, finely chopped

1 large tomato, seeded and diced

1 (15-ounce) can navy beans, rinsed and drained

½ teaspoon sea salt

½ teaspoon freshly ground black pepper

5 cups reduced-sodium vegetable broth

1 cup small pasta (such as tubetti)

2 tablespoons Marsala wine

2 bay leaves

FOR THE PISTOU

1 clove garlic, coarsely chopped

1 cup fresh baby spinach or arugula

½ cup packed fresh basil leaves

¼ cup toasted walnut pieces

3 tablespoons extra-virgin olive oil

2 tablespoons freshly squeezed lemon juice

2 teaspoons light miso paste

¼ teaspoon sea salt

½ teaspoon freshly ground black pepper

2 tablespoons vegan Parmesan, for topping (optional)

TO PREPARE THE SOUP

Heat a large saucepan over medium-low heat. Add oil, onion, and garlic. Sauté for 3 to 5 minutes, or until softened. Add zucchini, carrot, tomato, beans, sea salt, and pepper. Cook for 2 more minutes. Add broth, pasta, wine, and bay leaves. Stir to incorporate and cover. Cook for 20 to 25 minutes, or until pasta and vegetables are soft.

TO PREPARE THE PISTOU

Add garlic, spinach, basil, walnuts, oil, lemon juice, miso, sea salt, and pepper to a food processor or high-powered blender. Blend for 15 to 30 seconds, or until smooth.

Discard bay leaves before serving. Ladle warm soup into bowls and top with a generous dollop of pistou, and Parmesan, if desired.

TIP Marsala wine from Sicily is great for cooking because it won't break the bank. However, if you have an open bottle of red wine, just pop in 2 tablespoons in place of the Marsala and your soup will be equally delicious.

Red Lentil Soup with Almond Gremolata

GLUTEN-FREE

Serves 4 to 6

Prep time: 12 minutes

Cook time: 28 minutes

FOR THE GREMOLATA

1 cup packed fresh parsley, coarsely chopped

1 clove garlic, coarsely chopped

¼ cup toasted slivered almonds

¼ teaspoon red pepper flakes

⅛ teaspoon sea salt

2 tablespoons extra-virgin olive oil

1 tablespoon freshly squeezed lemon juice, plus zest of ½ lemon

Canada is the largest producer of lentils, a cold weather-loving crop, and our pals over in Saskatchewan grow well over 90 percent of the world's supply. Who knew? Red lentils are a particular variety that cook very quickly and are packed with iron. *Oh Canada!*

TO PREPARE THE GREMOLATA

In a food processor or blender, combine parsley, garlic, almonds, red pepper flakes, sea salt, oil, lemon juice and zest, and blend until uniform. Set aside.

TIP Unlike most beans and pulses, there's no need to soak lentils! When cooking them, just use 3 parts liquid to 1 part lentils, and in 18 to 20 minutes you'll be ready to roll.

FOR THE SOUP

1 tablespoon neutral-tasting oil

½ medium yellow onion,
finely chopped

2 cloves garlic, minced

1 large carrot, finely diced

1 stalk celery, finely diced

½ red bell pepper, finely chopped

½ teaspoon sea salt

½ teaspoon freshly ground
black pepper

2 cups dried red lentils

1 bay leaf

6 cups reduced-sodium
vegetable broth

1 cup water

3 tablespoons freshly squeezed
lemon juice

2 teaspoons brown rice syrup

TO PREPARE THE SOUP

1. Heat a large saucepan over medium heat. Add oil and sauté onion and garlic for 3 to 5 minutes, or until softened. Add carrot, celery, bell pepper, sea salt, and pepper and stir to coat. Cook for 3 to 5 more minutes.

2. Add lentils, bay leaf, broth, and water. Cook 16 to 18 minutes, or until lentils are soft enough to mash with a fork. Add lemon juice and brown rice syrup. Remove from heat and discard bay leaf.

3. Using an immersion blender, blend about half the batch of soup. Alternatively, blend half of the soup mixture in a blender, with middle of lid removed, covered in a clean kitchen towel.

4. Gently whisk together blended and unblended soup. Season with more sea salt and pepper, if desired. Ladle soup into bowls and top each serving with gremolata.

Split Pea Soup with Crumbled Tempeh Bacon

NUT-FREE

Serves 4 to 6

Prep time: 10 minutes

Cook time: 1 hour, 5 minutes

1 tablespoon neutral-tasting oil

1 yellow onion, finely chopped

2 cloves garlic, finely chopped

2 carrots, finely diced

2½ cups dried split peas

1 teaspoon dried oregano

½ teaspoon dried thyme

2 bay leaves

¼ teaspoon cayenne pepper

½ teaspoon sea salt

½ teaspoon freshly ground
   black pepper

6 cups reduced-sodium
   vegetable broth

1 tablespoon freshly squeezed
   lemon juice

1 teaspoon brown rice syrup

2 teaspoons vegan butter

4 to 6 strips, tempeh bacon,
   crumbled

Split peas may have been put on this earth just to make split pea soup. The way the peas thicken the soup but also retain a great texture is miraculous. This soup comes together quickly, and the addition of tempeh bacon adds a layer of comforting flavor that's like wearing a polar fleece vest over your cozy flannel shirt.

1. Heat a large saucepan over medium heat. Add oil and sauté onion, garlic, and carrots for 3 to 5 minutes, or until softened. Add split peas, oregano, thyme, bay leaves, cayenne, sea salt, pepper, and broth.

2. Bring soup to a boil and stir. Reduce heat to a simmer and cook for 45 minutes to 1 hour, or until split peas are tender. Remove from heat and discard bay leaves.

3. Add lemon juice and brown rice syrup. Using an immersion blender, blend about half the batch of soup. Alternatively, blend half soup mixture in a blender, with middle of lid removed, covered in a clean kitchen towel.

4. Heat a small skillet over medium heat and add butter. Add tempeh bacon and cook until crispy, about 4 minutes.

5. Serve the soup warm, topped with tempeh bacon crumbles.

TIP Not all veggie broth gives your soup delicious results. We've found our favorite is Imagine brand's No-Chicken Vegetarian Broth. It has a balanced flavor, and the richness we love. If you can't find it, just look for a vegetarian broth that isn't tomato-based.

Asian Sweet Corn Soup

GLUTEN-FREE · NUT-FREE

Serves 4 to 6

Prep time: 10 minutes

Cook time: 22 minutes

1 tablespoon neutral-tasting oil, plus 2 teaspoons, divided

3 cups fresh or frozen (thawed) corn kernels

3 cloves garlic, finely chopped

2 carrots, finely diced

1 shallot, finely chopped

1 teaspoon sea salt

½ teaspoon freshly ground black pepper

5 cups reduced-sodium vegetable broth

2 tablespoons soy milk creamer

1 tablespoon arrowroot powder

2 teaspoons toasted sesame oil

¼ cup scallions, thinly sliced

Want a quick soup to accompany an Asian meal? This is the one! The corn base provides sweetness, acts as a thickener, and is packed with a phytochemical called lutein, which may improve vision.

1. Heat a large pot over medium heat. Add 1 tablespoon neutral-tasting oil and cook corn about 5 minutes, until softened. Remove corn from pan and add to food processor. Blend until smooth and set aside.

2. To same large pot, add remaining 2 teaspoons neutral-tasting oil, garlic, carrots, and shallot. Sauté for 3 to 4 minutes, or until slightly softened. Add sea salt, pepper, broth, and blended corn. Reduce heat to a simmer and cook, partially covered, for 10 to 12 minutes.

3. In a small bowl, whisk creamer and arrowroot. Drizzle into soup and stir to thicken while cooking, about 1 minute.

4. Remove from heat. Drizzle soup with sesame oil and stir gently. Serve soup topped with scallions.

TIP You can make tea using corn silk from a fresh cob. Just steep the silk in warm water for about 10 minutes, strain out, and enjoy. The corn silk tea can help lower blood pressure and has been used to treat urinary tract infections.

Sweet and Smoky Red Bean Stew

NUT-FREE
Serves 4 to 6
Prep time: 15 minutes
Cook time: 25 minutes

1 tablespoon neutral-tasting oil

1 medium yellow onion, finely chopped

2 cloves garlic, finely chopped

1 orange or red bell pepper,
 finely diced

1 carrot, finely diced

4 strips tempeh bacon, diced

½ teaspoon dried oregano

½ teaspoon dried thyme

½ teaspoon sea salt

½ teaspoon freshly ground
 black pepper

2 (15-ounce) cans kidney beans,
 rinsed and drained

1 to 2 teaspoons hot sauce

2 tablespoons brown sugar

2 tablespoons red wine vinegar

3 tablespoons tomato paste

1 cup reduced-sodium
 vegetable broth

2 tablespoons fresh chives,
 finely chopped, for garnish

Give your beans a swift kick in the overalls with this real-deal, down-home stew. Ranch-style beans, or smoky beans, are a dish made with flavors of Texas. The tempeh bacon, brown sugar, tomato paste, and spices bring those flavors in. Whether you're a Boston Brahmin or a West Coast surfer, you'll want to fill your bowl to the brim with this taste of Southern hospitality.

1. Heat a 6-quart saucepan and add oil. Add onion, garlic, bell pepper, and carrot. Cook for 3 to 5 minutes, or until soft. Add tempeh bacon, oregano, thyme, sea salt, and pepper. Stir to incorporate.

2. Add beans, hot sauce, brown sugar, vinegar, tomato paste, and broth. Cook, uncovered, stirring occasionally, for 15 to 20 minutes, or until most liquid is absorbed, or desired thickness is reached. Serve warm, garnished with chives.

TIP A hefty helping of kidney beans can help regulate blood sugar after your meal, giving you sustained energy. Beans are good for diabetics, and their cholesterol-lowering fiber makes them a friend of your ticker, too.

TIP If you're serving this stew to a crowd, get a little fancy and top with a dollop of vegan sour cream and sliced radishes.

Wild Mushroom and Herb Soup with Brown Rice

GLUTEN-FREE • NUT-FREE
Serves 4 to 6
Prep time: 15 minutes
Cook time: 45 minutes

3 tablespoons vegan butter, divided

1 medium yellow onion, finely chopped

2 cloves garlic, finely chopped

1 carrot, finely chopped

2 stalks celery, finely chopped

1 tablespoon nutritional yeast

½ teaspoon sea salt, plus pinch

½ teaspoon freshly ground black pepper, plus pinch

¼ cup short-grain brown rice

6 cups reduced-sodium vegetable broth

1 bay leaf

1½ cups fresh cremini and/or oyster mushrooms, coarsely chopped

2 teaspoons fresh rosemary, stemmed and finely chopped

1 teaspoon fresh thyme, stemmed and finely chopped

2 teaspoons dry sherry

1 tablespoon freshly squeezed lemon juice, plus zest of 1 lemon

1 tablespoon fresh chives, finely chopped, for garnish

When you envision what soup would be served at your favorite mom-and-pop vegan restaurant, this one might be it. We've upped the sophistication in our version, but kept it warming and comforting, making it perfect for both casual nights in your pjs and fancy dinner parties.

1. Heat a large stockpot over medium heat. Add 2 tablespoons butter, onion, and garlic. Cook for 3 to 5 minutes, until softened. Add carrot, celery, nutritional yeast, sea salt, and pepper. Cook for 2 more minutes. Add rice and broth.

2. Reduce heat to a simmer, add bay leaf, and cook, partially covered, for 35 to 40 minutes, or until rice is soft.

3. Meanwhile, heat a skillet over medium heat and add remaining 1 tablespoon butter, mushrooms, rosemary, and thyme. Season with pinch sea salt and pepper. Add sherry. Cook about 6 minutes, or until golden.

4. Add mushrooms to soup, then add lemon juice and zest. Discard bay leaf. Season with more sea salt and pepper, if desired, and garnish with chives. Serve warm.

TIP Though short-grain brown rice takes longer to cook than long-grain, it's worth the wait in this soup for the texture. If you really need this soup quickly, you can purchase precooked short-grain brown rice and toss it in. Reduce the cooking time to 12 to 15 minutes.

Seitan Chowder

Serves 4 to 6
Prep time: 10 minutes
Cook time: 30 minutes

4 tablespoons vegan butter, divided

2 cups seitan (8 ounces), diced

¾ teaspoon sea salt, divided

½ teaspoon freshly ground black
pepper, divided

Zest of ½ lemon

¼ cup unbleached all-purpose flour

1 medium yellow onion, finely chopped

3 cloves garlic, finely chopped

1 carrot, finely chopped

1 stalk celery, finely chopped

1 russet potato, peeled and diced

3 slices tempeh bacon

2 tablespoons nutritional yeast

1 tablespoon freshly squeezed
lemon juice

4 cups unsweetened almond or
soy milk

1 cup reduced-sodium
vegetable broth

TIP Seitan has about 20 grams
of protein for a 3-ounce serving,
comparable to its meaty counterparts.

A vegan chowder is hard to find, which is why we included this recipe. New England popularized clam chowder, but there's no need for clams when you have delicious seitan at the ready. If you want an authentic experience, pair with flaky crackers alongside or crumbled on top.

1. Heat a sauté pan over medium heat. Melt 1 tablespoon butter. Add seitan, ¼ teaspoon sea salt, ¼ teaspoon pepper, and lemon zest. Cook about 4 minutes, or until seitan is browned. Set aside.

2. Heat a 4-quart saucepan over medium heat. Add remaining 3 tablespoons butter and flour and whisk to create a roux (a paste). Cook 1 minute, or until flour has a light toasted color and fragrance. Be careful not to burn. Add onion and garlic and sauté for about 2 minutes, or until slightly softened. Add carrot, celery, potato, tempeh bacon, nutritional yeast, remaining ½ teaspoon sea salt, and remaining ¼ teaspoon pepper. Cook for 3 to 4 more minutes. Add lemon juice, almond or soy milk, and broth.

3. Reduce heat to a simmer and cook, partially covered, for about 20 minutes, or until potatoes are very soft.

4. Blend 2 cups soup in a blender, with middle of lid removed and covered with a clean kitchen towel, to prevent spillage.

5. Add blended soup back to pot and add cooked seitan pieces. Season with more sea salt and pepper, if desired. Serve warm.

Recipe p.116

Handhelds

Ditch your spork and knife while eating your way through this chapter. Here, you'll find our favorite recipes from across the globe that can be eaten with just your mitts. These dishes are great for lunches, to enjoy at school or at work, picnics, parties, and informal evening dinners. Many of these dishes can be made gluten-free with a few easy swaps, so don't be afraid to experiment.

Our inspiration for items like the Tempeh Tuna Wrap, Argentinean Empanadas, and Battered Avocado Tacos comes from admiring dishes we've seen in restaurants while traveling. Dishes such as these are easy to veganize; all you need are the right tools. So wash your hands, roll up your sleeves, and start creating your own handheld masterpieces.

Baked Tofu-Avocado Hand Roll with Ginger-Tamari Sauce

Go-To Recipe

GLUTEN-FREE · NUT-FREE

Makes 6 to 8 hand rolls

Prep time: 35 minutes

Cook time: 25 to 35 minutes

FOR THE RICE

1 cup sushi rice (or brown rice)

2 tablespoons rice vinegar

1 tablespoon evaporated cane sugar

½ teaspoon sea salt

FOR THE FILLING

1 (6-ounce) block gluten-free baked tofu, cut into thin matchsticks

½ ripe avocado, peeled and cut into thin segments

½ red or orange bell pepper, cut into thin matchsticks

1 carrot, cut into long strips

1 Persian (or ¼ English) cucumber, halved and cut into thin strips

4 toasted nori sheets, halved

2 tablespoons wasabi powder mixed with 1 tablespoon water (optional)

½ cup pickled ginger

TIP Not all wasabi powder and paste is vegan. Search the label carefully for any added dairy.

This hand roll has all the flavors of a veggie sushi roll but takes half the time to prepare. The best part? It's so much fun forming the sushi—it is edible art, after all. Plus, there are so many different fillings you can add to your hand roll, making it a great addition to an impromptu dinner party. The best-best part is that you get to enjoy it with a glass of your favorite cold Japanese beer or hot sake, depending on the weather.

TO PREPARE THE RICE

Cook rice according to package directions. When cooked, transfer to a large bowl. With a wooden paddle, incorporate vinegar, sugar, and sea salt into rice until slightly sticky. Set aside to cool.

TO PREPARE THE FILLING

Arrange tofu, avocado, bell pepper, carrot, and cucumber on a plate within easy reach.

TO FORM THE HAND ROLLS

1. Place 1 piece nori (shiny-side down) in one hand. With dampened other hand, spread about ¼ cup cooked sushi rice evenly over half the nori in a square.

2. Place small amount of desired fillings in a diagonal line across rice, pointing toward thumb.

3. Gently roll into a cone shape and seal edge with a few grains of sushi rice or with prepared wasabi (if using). Serve with ginger.

FOR THE GINGER-TAMARI SAUCE

½ cup vegan mayonnaise

2 teaspoons tamari

2 teaspoons fresh ginger, grated

2 teaspoons rice vinegar

1 teaspoon brown rice syrup

¼ teaspoon sea salt

¼ teaspoon freshly ground
  black pepper

TO PREPARE THE GINGER-TAMARI SAUCE

1. Whisk mayonnaise, tamari, ginger, vinegar, brown rice syrup, sea salt, and pepper in a bowl until uniform.

2. Drizzle sauce over hand rolls and serve with pickled ginger and wasabi.

TIP Don't overstuff your sushi! It's a beginner's mistake to get overzealous and fill your hand roll to the brim. You'll make it very difficult to seal and eat.

Japanese Yam Hand Roll

1 small Japanese yam, unpeeled
2 teaspoons black sesame seeds

1. Make rice as written in original recipe.

2. Preheat oven to 375°F. Roast yam for 45 minutes, or until soft. When cool, peel and cut into 2-inch-thick strips. Set aside.

3. Arrange filling ingredients as directed in original recipe, substituting yam and sesame seeds for tofu and carrot. Form rolls as directed in original recipe.

4. Drizzle with either Ginger-Tamari Sauce from original recipe or Creamy Miso Sauce from variation.

Glazed Shiitake Hand Roll with Creamy Miso Sauce

FOR THE MUSHROOMS

2 teaspoons neutral-tasting oil

6 large shiitake mushrooms, stemmed and thinly sliced

1 teaspoon tamari

1 teaspoon brown rice syrup

2 teaspoons rice vinegar

1 package enoki mushrooms, ends trimmed

FOR THE CREAMY MISO SAUCE

2 tablespoons light miso paste

1 teaspoon rice vinegar

2 teaspoons toasted sesame oil

1½ tablespoons vegan mayonnaise

1 teaspoon evaporated cane sugar

¼ teaspoon sea salt

1 tablespoon unsweetened almond milk

1. Make rice as written in original recipe.

2. To make mushrooms, heat a small skillet and add neutral-tasting oil. Add shiitake mushrooms, tamari, brown rice syrup, and vinegar and cook until mushrooms are golden brown, about 3 to 5 minutes. Let cool and place in a small bowl.

3. Arrange filling ingredients as directed in original recipe, substituting glazed shiitake and fresh enoki mushrooms for tofu. Form rolls as directed in original recipe.

4. Whisk together all Creamy Miso Sauce ingredients and drizzle over hand rolls.

Philadelphia Hand Roll

½ (4-ounce) container vegan cream cheese

1 roasted red bell pepper, cut into ½-inch-thick strips

¼ cup toasted cashew pieces

¼ teaspoon smoked sea salt

1. Make rice as written in original recipe.

2. Arrange filling ingredients as directed in original recipe, substituting cream cheese, roasted bell pepper, cashew pieces, and smoked sea salt for tofu, raw bell pepper, and shredded carrot. Form rolls as directed in original recipe. No sauce is necessary for this hand roll.

TIP The roasted red bell pepper and smoked sea salt makes a great substitute for smoked salmon. You can find smoked sea salt at gourmet markets, some natural foods stores, or online.

Tempeh Tuna Salad Wrap

GLUTEN-FREE

30 MINUTES OR LESS

Serves 4 to 6

Prep time: 15 minutes

Cook time: 15 minutes

1 (8-ounce) package soy tempeh, cut into 6 to 8 slices

1 tablespoon neutral-tasting oil

1 shallot, finely chopped

⅓ cup vegan mayonnaise

2 tablespoons freshly squeezed lemon juice

2 teaspoons whole-grain or stone-ground mustard

2 kosher dill pickles, finely chopped

½ cup grated carrots

¼ cup fresh dill, finely chopped

2 tablespoons almonds or cashews, coarsely chopped

1 tablespoon capers, drained

½ teaspoon sea salt

½ teaspoon freshly ground black pepper

1 head butter lettuce, large leaves only

1 tablespoon red bell pepper, finely diced (optional)

We think you'll be singing to the tun-a this wrap in no time at all. High-protein, nutty tempeh welcomes lemon pickle relish, vegan mayo, and more, becoming the catch of the day.

1. Fill a pot with about an inch of water and place a steamer basket in pot. Bring to a simmer with lid on. Steam tempeh for 5 to 7 minutes. Set aside to cool slightly.

2. Heat a sauté pan over medium heat. Add oil and shallot and sauté for about 2 minutes. Crumble tempeh in your hands and add to pan. Cook for about 5 minutes, until well browned. Set aside to cool, about 10 minutes.

3. In a large bowl, combine mayonnaise, lemon juice, mustard, pickles, carrots, dill, almonds or cashews, capers, sea salt, and pepper. When tempeh has cooled, add to bowl and mix well.

4. On a tray or large plate, arrange lettuce cups in a single layer. To form the wraps, add about ¼ cup tempeh salad to each lettuce cup. Top with bell pepper (if using).

TIP Why steam tempeh? It removes any bitterness the tempeh may have, and opens it up to accepting flavors.

Cucumber-Dill Finger Sandwiches with Homemade Walnut Cream Cheese

30 MINUTES OR LESS

Makes 4 large or 12 small sandwiches

Prep time: 10 minutes

Cook time: 2 minutes

1 cup plus 2 tablespoons walnut pieces

⅛ teaspoon garlic powder

¼ teaspoon sea salt, plus ⅛ teaspoon, divided

½ teaspoon evaporated cane sugar

1 tablespoon neutral-tasting oil

¼ cup unsweetened almond milk

1½ tablespoons freshly squeezed lemon juice

½ teaspoon light miso paste

½ hothouse cucumber, cut into thin rounds

⅛ teaspoon freshly ground black pepper

8 slices white or spelt bread

2 tablespoons fresh dill, finely chopped

It doesn't have to be teatime for you to enjoy these delectable little treats; they're delicious 'round the clock. The walnut cream cheese is nutrient rich and decadent while the cucumbers and dill add a light, complementary coolness. So pour yourself some tea, practice your pinky pointing, and have a sandwich.

1. In a food processor or high-powered blender, combine walnuts, garlic powder, ¼ teaspoon sea salt, sugar, oil, almond milk, lemon juice, and miso. Blend until smooth and creamy.

2. Sprinkle sliced cucumbers with remaining ⅛ teaspoon sea salt and pepper. Set aside.

3. Lightly toast bread in toaster, about 2 minutes. Spread each slice with about 1 tablespoon walnut cream cheese. Add cucumbers to 4 slices of bread. Top with dill and enclose with remaining slices of bread.

4. Cut off crusts, if desired, and slice diagonally to create large triangles, or cut into three rectangular pieces per sandwich.

TIP If you are making these finger sandwiches in advance for a party, cover with wax paper, then top with a slightly damp paper towel to keep them in tip-top shape.

Quick and Easy Red Bean Veggie Burgers

NUT-FREE · 30 MINUTES OR LESS
Makes 4 to 6 patties
Prep time: 10 minutes
Cook time: 10 minutes

---

1 (15-ounce) can kidney beans, rinsed and drained

1 teaspoon dried minced onion

¼ teaspoon garlic powder

¾ teaspoon sea salt

½ teaspoon freshly ground black pepper

3 tablespoons vegan Worcestershire sauce

2 tablespoons freshly squeezed lemon juice

1 tablespoon brown rice syrup

½ cup rolled oats

½ cup unbleached flour or cornmeal

1 to 2 tablespoons neutral-tasting oil

4 to 6 vegan buns, split

4 to 6 (4-inch square) pieces romaine lettuce

4 to 6 slices tomato

Choice of ketchup, mustard, pickle relish, barbecue sauce, or other toppings

Beans are one of the vegan foods that wear many hats. They can disguise themselves as burgers, dips, and even meringue. We use red beans as the main ingredient in this burger because the color is spot on, the texture comes out meaty (in the most vegan-y way possible), and it's a fantastic base for a wide variety of toppings.

1. In a food processor, combine beans, onion, garlic powder, sea salt, pepper, Worcestershire sauce, lemon juice, and brown rice syrup. Pulse 5 times. Add oats and flour or cornmeal, and pulse until mixture holds together.

2. Heat a large skillet and add oil. With damp hands, form the burger mixture into patties and place in pan. Cook for 3 to 5 minutes on each side, or until browned.

3. Toast buns until golden. Place a burger on each bun bottom, top with lettuce, tomato, other desired toppings, and remaining bun half.

TIP Always thoroughly rinse and drain canned beans. They're much more digestible after the bubbles are washed away and will prevent your belly from hurting.

Buffalo Tofu Wraps

Serves 4 to 6
Prep time: 15 minutes
Cook time: 18 minutes

Fire drill! It's time to stop, drop, and roll. This sauce is not for anyone we would affectionately call a "spice wimp," because it can pack a punch. But don't fear, once you drop the tofu into your wrap and roll it into a tortilla, the spiciness mellows out a little.

FOR THE TOFU

1 (20-ounce) container extra-firm tofu, drained, pressed, and cut into ½-inch-thick strips

¼ cup unsweetened almond milk

1 tablespoon freshly squeezed lime juice

¼ cup whole-wheat pastry flour

¼ cup unbleached all-purpose flour

½ teaspoon sea salt

¼ teaspoon freshly ground black pepper

½ teaspoon garlic powder

¼ teaspoon dried oregano

1 tablespoon neutral-tasting oil

TO PREPARE THE TOFU

1. Place tofu in a bowl with almond milk and lime juice and toss to coat.

2. In a separate bowl, whisk flours, sea salt, pepper, garlic powder, and oregano.

3. Heat a sauté pan over medium heat and add oil. Toss tofu in flour mixture then sauté for about 4 minutes per side, or until golden. Set aside.

FOR THE BUFFALO SAUCE

2 tablespoons vegan butter

3 fresh Fresno peppers,
 seeded and diced

½ yellow onion, finely chopped

1 cup fresh mango, diced

¾ teaspoon sea salt

½ teaspoon ground paprika

Pinch nutmeg

½ teaspoon celery seed

½ teaspoon dried parsley flakes

¼ cup soy milk creamer

2 tablespoons apple cider vinegar

½ cup water

FOR THE WRAPS

6 to 8 large flour tortillas

3 cups shredded romaine lettuce

¼ red onion, cut into thin strips

¼ cup vegan sour cream (optional),
 for topping

TO PREPARE THE BUFFALO SAUCE

Add butter to pan and sauté peppers and onion, about 3 minutes. Add mango, sea salt, paprika, nutmeg, celery seed, parsley, creamer, vinegar, and water. Cook for 8 to 10 minutes, stirring frequently. Purée in blender until smooth.

TO FORM THE WRAPS

Add 2 or 3 pieces tofu to each tortilla. Top with lettuce, a few slices onion, and sour cream (if using). Roll into burrito shape and cut on a diagonal through middle. Serve with buffalo sauce on side.

TIP Fresno peppers are a thin-walled variety of spicy chile that pack a nice punch of heat. Because they're more fragile, you can't find a dried powder version of this chile, but you can always sub them out for red jalapeños.

Spicy Kale Caesar Roll-Ups

30 MINUTES OR LESS

Makes 4 (6-inch) roll-ups

Prep time: 15 minutes

FOR THE DRESSING

⅓ cup extra-virgin olive oil

2 tablespoons freshly squeezed lemon juice

1 tablespoon vegan Worcestershire sauce

2 teaspoons brown rice syrup

1 red jalapeño or Fresno pepper, seeded and coarsely chopped

1 clove garlic, coarsely chopped

¼ cup toasted pecan pieces

¼ cup nutritional yeast

½ teaspoon sea salt

¼ teaspoon freshly ground black pepper

½ teaspoon kelp granules

FOR THE ROLL-UPS

7 ounces baby kale

4 pieces lavash bread

1 avocado, peeled and cut into thin strips

1 tomato, diced

1 carrot, shredded (about ½ cup)

1 (6-ounce) package baked tofu, cut into ¼-inch-thick strips

¼ cup sliced almonds

Most people will agree that Caesar dressing can make just about anything taste good, and we think kale is a terrific vehicle for dressing. Mixing these two up is extremely delicious, and tucking them into a soft lavash bed together, along with a little heat, forms a cozy and flavorful handheld. We serve these at parties with frilly toothpicks, and now we're officially inviting you to do the same.

TO PREPARE THE DRESSING

In a high-powered blender or food processor, combine oil, lemon juice, Worcestershire sauce, brown rice syrup, red jalapeño or Fresno pepper, garlic, pecans, nutritional yeast, sea salt, pepper, and kelp granules. Blend until creamy and uniform. Set aside.

TO PREPARE THE ROLL-UPS

1. Toss baby kale with desired amount of dressing. Reserve ¼ cup dressing for rolling the pinwheels.

2. Place a small amount of dressing along top of one long edge of lavash. Place handful of kale toward the middle.

3. Top with a few slices of avocado, 1 tablespoon tomato, 2 tablespoons shredded carrot, a few strips tofu, and 1 tablespoon almonds. Roll lavash to make a long cylinder, sealing top by pressing gently. Slice each roll-up in half. Repeat for all roll-ups.

TIP If you don't like the heat, leave out the fresh chiles and sub in ½ teaspoon smoked paprika for added flavor.

Crunchy Asian Tofu and Veggie Lettuce Cups

GLUTEN-FREE

Serves 4 to 6

Prep time: 15 minutes,
plus 20 minutes to marinate

Cook time: 10 minutes

FOR THE SAUCE

2 tablespoons agave or maple syrup

2 tablespoons rice vinegar

2 tablespoons tamari

2 teaspoons toasted sesame oil

2 teaspoons fresh ginger, finely grated

Standard stir-fries are an easy meal choice for a busy weeknight, and serving them in lettuce cups adds an extra bit of fun. The carrot-bell pepper-water chestnut crunch paired with the tangy marinade and topped with the complex sauce is such a great combination, you'll be adding this to your regular arsenal.

TO PREPARE THE SAUCE

Combine agave or maple syrup, vinegar, tamari, oil, and ginger in a bowl and whisk. Set aside.

TIP We use tamari in this recipe because the flavor is even more rich and complex than soy sauce. It was originally a by-product from the fermentation of miso, giving it that deep flavor, and is packed with amino acids. Plus, it's gluten-free!

→

Crunchy Asian Tofu and Veggie Lettuce Cups *continued*

FOR THE FILLING

2 tablespoons rice vinegar

2 tablespoons tamari

2 teaspoons evaporated cane sugar

¼ teaspoon sea salt

½ teaspoon freshly ground
   black pepper

1 tablespoon fresh ginger, finely grated

1 (10-ounce) container extra-firm
   tofu, drained and pressed, diced

1 tablespoon neutral-tasting oil

1 orange or red bell pepper,
   finely diced

1 to 2 carrots, finely diced

1 can water chestnuts,
   drained and coarsely chopped

1 teaspoon toasted sesame oil

Juice and zest of 1 lime

3 tablespoons toasted
   slivered almonds

1 head butter lettuce,
   bottom sliced off

Sesame seeds, for garnish (optional)

2 scallions, cut into rounds (optional)

TO PREPARE THE FILLING

1. In a large bowl, add vinegar, tamari, sugar, sea salt, pepper, and ginger and whisk. Add tofu and set aside to marinate, about 20 minutes.

2. Meanwhile, heat a sauté pan over medium heat. Add neutral-tasting oil, tofu with all marinating liquid, bell pepper, carrots, and water chestnuts. Sauté about 3 minutes and add sesame oil and lime zest and juice. Cook for 5 to 7 minutes, or until tofu is golden. Add almonds and cook for 1 more minute.

3. On a large plate or tray, arrange lettuce leaves in a single layer. Fill each lettuce cup with a small amount of tofu filling and top with sauce. Garnish with sesame seeds and scallions (if using).

Baja Battered Avocado Tacos with Pickled Red Onions

Makes 8 tacos

Prep time: 15 minutes, plus
1 hour to overnight for onions

Cook time: 8 minutes

When you batter avocado slices, you create a crunch on the outside and a softness on the inside. This balance of textures, all wrapped up in a tortilla, will make you forget the until-now irresistible bottomless basket of tortilla chips.

FOR THE PICKLED ONIONS

½ cup red wine vinegar

2 tablespoons evaporated cane sugar

1½ cups warm water

½ teaspoon dried oregano

1 teaspoon sea salt

1 red onion, cut into thin strips

1 cinnamon stick

FOR THE BATTERED AVOCADO

½ cup unbleached all-purpose flour

½ teaspoon aluminum-free baking powder

½ teaspoon dried minced onion

¼ teaspoon sea salt

¼ teaspoon garlic powder

¼ teaspoon cayenne pepper

¼ teaspoon ground cumin

¼ cup plus 2 tablespoons unsweetened almond milk

1 tablespoon freshly squeezed lemon juice

3 tablespoons neutral-tasting oil, plus 2 teaspoons, divided

1 large avocado, peeled and cut into strips

FOR THE TACOS

8 corn tortillas

1½ cups green or red cabbage, finely shredded (¼ head cabbage)

2 tablespoons vegan sour cream

TO PREPARE THE PICKLED ONIONS

Place vinegar and sugar in a bowl. Add water and whisk to dissolve sugar. Add oregano and sea salt. Add onion and toss to coat, submerging completely in liquid. Add cinnamon stick and cover. Place in refrigerator for 1 hour to overnight.

TO PREPARE THE BATTERED AVOCADO

1. In a large bowl, add flour, baking powder, onion, sea salt, garlic powder, cayenne, cumin, almond milk, lemon juice, and 2 teaspoons oil. Whisk until uniform. Set aside.

2. Heat a small sauté pan over medium-high heat and add remaining 3 tablespoons oil.

3. Cut avocado into 8 even pieces. Dip slices into batter. Add battered avocado to pan and cook for about 3 minutes per side, until golden.

TO PREPARE THE TACOS

Heat tortillas on a warm skillet until pliable. Fill with 1 piece battered avocado and garnish with green or red cabbage, sour cream, and a few pickled onions. Serve immediately.

TIP To reduce the need for oil, use a nonstick pan to cook the battered avocados.

Fresh Tomato and Basil Pizzettes

NUT-FREE

Makes 8 (4-inch) round pizzettes

Prep time: 10 minutes

Cook time: 26 minutes

1 package vegan puff pastry
(2 [9-inch] sheets)

½ cup pizza sauce

24 fresh basil leaves

8 slices vegan mozzarella
cheese, quartered

1 large tomato, cut into thin rounds

¼ teaspoon sea salt

¼ teaspoon freshly ground
black pepper

2 teaspoons neutral-tasting oil,
for drizzling

TIP For a gourmet twist, use a scalloped 4-inch circular cookie cutter on the puff pastry. It looks beautiful and gives your pizzettes a great texture.

When you want all the flavors of pizza but don't want to wait for your dough to rise, these scrumptious personal rounds will fit the bill. Think of them as a fancy treat that's a couple notches above a pizza bagel. They're fully customizable, so add your favorite toppings and give them your stamp of approval.

1. Thaw puff pastry sheets before using, according to package directions.

2. Preheat oven to 425°F.

3. Cut each sheet of puff pastry into 4 large disks using 4-inch circular cookie cutter. Place disks on parchment-lined baking sheet.

4. Spoon 1 heaping tablespoon pizza sauce on each round of puff pastry, and spread out almost to edges.

5. Top each pizzette with 3 leaves fresh basil, 4 pieces cheese, and 1 slice tomato. Sprinkle pizzettes with sea salt and pepper. Drizzle each pizzette with oil.

6. Bake for about 26 minutes, or until golden.

Argentinean Empanadas

NUT-FREE

Makes about 8

Prep time: 20 minutes

Cook time: 30 minutes

FOR THE FILLING

1 tablespoon neutral-tasting oil

2 cloves garlic, finely chopped

1 small carrot, finely chopped

½ white onion, finely chopped

6 ounces vegan meat crumbles

½ teaspoon dried oregano

¼ teaspoon ground cumin

¼ teaspoon smoked paprika

¼ teaspoon sea salt

¼ teaspoon freshly ground
  black pepper

1 tablespoon freshly squeezed
  lemon juice

2 teaspoons white wine vinegar

¼ cup packed golden raisins

⅓ cup green olives, finely diced

Argentinean cuisine tends to successfully combine ingredients that wouldn't normally be caught in a room together. We used that concept to stuff olives, raisins, and unique spices into a flaky dough to create these crunchy little South American bundles of joy.

Preheat oven to 400°F.

TO PREPARE THE FILLING

Heat a sauté pan over medium heat and add oil. Add garlic, carrot, onion, meat crumbles, oregano, cumin, paprika, sea salt, and pepper, and sauté for about 5 minutes. Add lemon juice and vinegar, and cook for about 3 more minutes. Fold in raisins and olives and set aside to cool.

FOR THE DOUGH

⅓ cup vegan butter

⅓ cup vegan cream cheese

½ cup whole-wheat pastry flour

1 cup unbleached all-purpose flour

½ teaspoon aluminum-free
  baking powder

½ teaspoon sea salt

1 teaspoon evaporated cane sugar

2 tablespoons soy milk creamer,
  plus 2 teaspoons, divided

TO PREPARE THE DOUGH

In the bowl of a standing mixer or in a large bowl, combine butter and cream cheese. Blend together until uniform. Add flours, baking powder, sea salt, sugar, and 2 tablespoons creamer. Whisk until smooth and uniform, about 3 minutes. Don't overmix, as this will make dough tough.

TO PREPARE THE EMPANADAS

1. Grease a rimmed baking sheet.

2. Flour a surface and roll dough into 4-inch circles, ⅛ inch thick. Scraps may be re-rolled once to yield more empanadas.

3. Place 2 tablespoons filling in one dough round and fold into a half circle shape over filling. Press with a fork to seal around edges, using water if needed. Repeat for remaining rounds and filling. Brush tops with remaining 2 teaspoons creamer.

4. Place on greased baking sheet and bake for about 22 minutes, or until golden.

TIP The word *empanada* is derived from *empanar,* meaning "to enclose" in Spanish, but many countries have their own spin on this dish. From India, to Belize, to the Philippines, and even Sicily, each corner of the globe has an abundance of sweet and savory dough-wrapped goodies.

Thai Salad Rolls with Tangy Peanut Vinaigrette

GLUTEN-FREE

30 MINUTES OR LESS

Makes 4 to 6 rolls

Prep time: 25 minutes

It's so much more fun to eat your greens when they're rolled up in a chewy rice wrapper for you to grip, dip, and munch. This Thai-inspired dish requires minimal assembly, but tastes like you've honed your cooking skills in Bangkok for years.

FOR THE ROLLS

1 head red leaf or butter lettuce, shredded (about 3 cups)

1 teaspoon brown rice syrup or agave

1 teaspoon rice vinegar

1 teaspoon toasted sesame oil

½ teaspoon tamari

1 (6-ounce) block gluten-free baked tofu, cut into thin strips

1 carrot, finely grated or cut into thin strips

1 Persian (or ¼ English) cucumber, cut into thin strips

½ red or orange bell pepper, cut into thin strips

8 to 10 fresh mint leaves

4 to 6 dry spring roll rice wrappers (square or round banh trang)

1. In a large bowl, toss lettuce with brown rice syrup or agave, vinegar, oil, and tamari. Set aside.

2. Place tofu, carrot, cucumber, bell pepper, and mint in separate bowls or on a platter.

3. To roll, soak each rice wrapper in warm water 5 to 10 seconds, or until slightly softened. Place on a flat working surface and fill with a line of desired fillings, using lettuce as main filling, close to base of wrapper (if using square wrappers, have one tip pointing at you).

FOR THE VINAIGRETTE

¼ cup smooth unsweetened peanut butter

2 tablespoons hot water

1 to 2 tablespoons freshly squeezed lime juice

1 tablespoon maple syrup

1 tablespoon tamari

1 tablespoon rice vinegar

1 teaspoon toasted sesame oil

1 tablespoon pickled ginger, finely chopped

¼ teaspoon red pepper flakes

4. Begin by folding the bottom flap over filling. Bring two sides over folded bottom flap and then bring remaining side over entire roll, to create a burrito shape. Squeeze to ensure filling is compacted. Set aside and repeat for all rolls. Slice rolls on a bias.

5. To make vinaigrette, in a bowl, add peanut butter and hot water. Whisk until uniform. Add lime juice, maple syrup, tamari, vinegar, oil, ginger, and red pepper flakes. Whisk until uniform. Serve rolls with vinaigrette on the side.

TIP Don't make these too far in advance. If you refrigerate rice wrappers, they become hard and lose their chewy texture.

Quesadillas with Creamy Chipotle Bean Dip and Charred Onion Salsa

NUT-FREE

Serves 4 to 6

Prep time: 15 minutes

Cook time: 18 minutes

FOR THE QUESADILLAS

2 teaspoons neutral-tasting oil

4 large flour tortillas

1 cup shredded vegan Pepper Jack cheese

FOR THE BEAN DIP

2 (16-ounce) cans pinto beans, rinsed and drained

½ cup vegan chipotle mayonnaise

2 tablespoons freshly squeezed lime juice

2 teaspoons agave or brown rice syrup

½ teaspoon sea salt

FOR THE SALSA

½ red onion, skin on

1 teaspoon neutral-tasting oil

¼ cup fresh or frozen (thawed) corn kernels

½ teaspoon sea salt

¼ teaspoon freshly ground black pepper

2 tablespoons freshly squeezed lime juice

2 teaspoons agave

1 tablespoon fresh cilantro, coarsely chopped

Cook like every day is Super Bowl Sunday. This dip can tag along while tailgating, accompany you to a friend's house party, or snuggle up with you on the couch while watching TV. The bean dip is perfect for your quesadilla wedges, but if that sounds like too much effort, just grab a bag of tortilla chips and go to town.

TO PREPARE THE QUESADILLAS

Heat a griddle over medium heat. Add oil. Add 1 or 2 tortillas at a time and sprinkle each tortilla with ½ cup cheese. Cook about 3 to 4 minutes, or until golden. Enclose with remaining tortillas, flip, and cook 3 to 4 more minutes, or until golden. Set aside to cool slightly and cut into triangles.

TO PREPARE THE DIP

In a food processor, purée all dip ingredients until smooth and set aside.

TO PREPARE THE SALSA

On a medium open flame, place the flat side of onion and char until blackened, 3 to 5 minutes. When slightly cooled, peel, cut into small dice and set aside. In a small skillet, heat oil. Add corn and cook 3 to 5 minutes, or until golden. Place in a mixing bowl and add sea salt, pepper, lime juice, agave, and cilantro. Add charred onion.

To serve, place dip in a serving bowl, top with salsa, and serve quesadilla wedges on the side for dipping.

TIP Give your quesadilla a little extra crisping time in the pan to get that restaurant-quality crunch and golden color. It's worth the effort and helps hold its structure for dipping.

Pimento Cheese and Sautéed Spinach Panini

30 MINUTES OR LESS

Makes 4 sandwiches

Prep time: 10 minutes

Cook time: 6 minutes

FOR THE PIMENTO CHEESE

½ cup raw cashews

¼ teaspoon garlic powder

¼ teaspoon sea salt

1 teaspoon agave

1 teaspoon neutral-tasting oil

3 tablespoons unsweetened almond or soy milk

1 tablespoon freshly squeezed lemon juice

½ teaspoon vegan Worcestershire sauce

⅛ teaspoon cayenne pepper

¼ cup jarred pimentos, drained and chopped

2 tablespoons vegan cream cheese

FOR THE SPINACH

1 tablespoon extra-virgin olive oil

4 cups baby spinach

1 tablespoon freshly squeezed lemon juice

¼ teaspoon sea salt

¼ teaspoon freshly ground black pepper

1 teaspoon vegan butter

6 slices sourdough or whole-wheat bread

This would be Popeye's perfect panini. It has a ton of his favorite greens, mixed with a cashew-based pimento cheese that works like a dream when pressed between layers of fresh bread.

TO PREPARE THE PIMENTO CHEESE

In a large food processor or high-powered blender, add cashews, garlic powder, sea salt, agave, neutral-tasting oil, almond or soy milk, lemon juice, Worcestershire sauce, and cayenne. Blend until smooth and uniform. Transfer to a bowl and fold in pimentos and cream cheese.

TO PREPARE THE SPINACH

Heat a small skillet over medium-low heat. Add olive oil and spinach. Cook about 2 minutes, or until slightly wilted. Add lemon juice, sea salt, and pepper and cook about 1 more minute, or until spinach is completely wilted. Drain off excess liquid. Set aside.

TO ASSEMBLE THE PANINI

1. Heat panini press and add butter. Spread pimento cheese on 3 slices bread and top each slice with cooked spinach. Enclose with remaining slices bread.

2. Place 1 or 2 sandwiches in panini press at a time, depending on size of press. Toast until golden, about 3 to 4 minutes.

TIP Pimentos are small, sweet, and tart peppers, famous for being stuffed in green olives. Use them instead of red bell peppers in any recipe where you want to add a unique flavor.

Cheesy and Saucy Italian Meatball Sub

NUT-FREE • 30 MINUTES OR LESS

Makes 4 sandwiches

Prep time: 12 minutes

Cook time: 14 minutes

1 (8-ounce) package tempeh, thickly sliced

2 tablespoons freshly squeezed lemon juice

1 tablespoon stone-ground mustard

2 teaspoons brown rice syrup

½ teaspoon sea salt

¼ teaspoon freshly ground black pepper

¼ teaspoon red pepper flakes

1 tablespoon fresh parsley, plus 2 teaspoons, finely chopped, divided

1 teaspoon fennel seeds

½ cup bread crumbs

1 tablespoon neutral-tasting oil

2 cups marinara sauce

6 slices vegan provolone cheese, cut into triangles

4 (5-inch) sandwich rolls, sliced horizontally

1 tablespoon vegan Parmesan, for topping (optional)

TIP Tempeh is made by fermentation, an ancient method of preserving food. Other examples of fermented foods include cider, yogurt, sauerkraut, beer, kombucha, kimchi, and pickles.

A messy, saucy sub is one of the most fun sandwiches to eat. We love grabbing a large stack of napkins and diving into this flavorful handheld that's *almost* too big. The bread really helps make this a winner, so be sure to get nice, fresh, fluffy Italian rolls.

1. Fill a 4-quart saucepan with about 1 inch of water and place a steamer basket in pot. Bring to a simmer with a lid on. Place tempeh in pot and steam for about 7 minutes. Remove from heat and cool slightly.

2. In a food processor, combine steamed tempeh, lemon juice, mustard, brown rice syrup, sea salt, black pepper, red pepper flakes, 2 teaspoons parsley, fennel seeds, and bread crumbs. Pulse about 30 times, until mixture is uniform. Scoop out 2 tablespoons tempeh mixture and form into a ball. Repeat to make 12 meatballs.

3. Heat a large nonstick skillet over medium heat and add oil. Add meatballs and cook on all sides, for about 2 minutes per side, or until golden, shaking pan occasionally to help rotate meatballs.

4. Heat marinara sauce in small saucepan over medium-low heat until warmed through, about 3 minutes. Set aside.

5. To form sandwich, place 3 cheese triangles on bottom half of each roll. Add 3 meatballs to each roll and slather with marinara sauce. Top with remaining parsley, Parmesan (if using), and roll tops.

French Dip Sandwiches with Walnut Jus

Serves 4 to 6

Prep time: 18 minutes,
plus 20 minutes to marinate

Cook time: 20 minutes

FOR THE SEITAN FILLING

1 (8-ounce) package seitan

2 tablespoons brown rice syrup

2 tablespoons sherry vinegar

2 tablespoons vegan
Worcestershire sauce

½ teaspoon sea salt

¼ teaspoon freshly ground
black pepper

1 tablespoon neutral-tasting oil

1 shallot, finely chopped

1 yellow onion, thinly sliced

6 to 8 cremini mushrooms,
thinly sliced

Believe it or not, the French dip sandwich was invented in Los Angeles. Our mushroom and seitan version is a lighter take on this sandwich that's usually just meat between bread. And as a bonus, instead of the usual side-cup of watery beef jus, you'll get to dip this puppy in a hot and hearty homemade gravy.

TO PREPARE THE FILLING

1. Slice seitan into thin strips by hand or with slicing blade attachment in food processor. Transfer to a large bowl. Add brown rice syrup, vinegar, Worcestershire sauce, sea salt, and pepper. Toss to coat and marinate 10 to 20 minutes.

2. Preheat a large sauté pan over medium heat and add oil. Add shallot and onion and sauté for about 3 minutes, or until soft. Add mushrooms and sauté for an additional 3 minutes. Add marinated seitan and cook about 5 to 7 minutes, or until golden. Remove from pan and set aside.

3. Preheat oven to 350°F.

FOR THE WALNUT JUS

2 tablespoons unbleached all-purpose flour

1 tablespoon neutral-tasting oil

2 cups chicken-style vegetable broth

1 tablespoon sherry vinegar

1 tablespoon vegan Worcestershire sauce

2 teaspoons evaporated cane sugar

½ teaspoon sea salt

¼ teaspoon freshly ground black pepper

¼ cup toasted walnuts, coarsely chopped

4 to 6 vegan French rolls

TO MAKE THE WALNUT JUS

Add flour and oil to pan used for seitan. Whisk to form a roux (a paste). Cook 1 minute, or until flour has a light toasted color and fragrance. Be careful not to burn. Add broth, vinegar, Worcestershire sauce, sugar, sea salt, and pepper. Cook over medium heat, whisking frequently, until sauce thickens slightly, 5 to 7 minutes. Add walnuts and stir.

Slice rolls in half and toast in oven for 3 minutes to warm.

To serve, place seitan mixture on roll bottoms and top with roll tops. Fill small ramekins with ⅓ to ½ cup warm jus and serve with sandwiches.

TIP Walnuts are anti-inflammatory and good for your cardiovascular system; they contain a certain type of vitamin E that may protect against heart problems.

CBLTA (Carrot Bacon, Lettuce, Tomato, and Avocado)

NUT-FREE

Serves 4

Prep time: 15 minutes

Cook time: 24 minutes

FOR THE CARROT BACON

3 large carrots

2 tablespoons neutral-tasting oil

2 teaspoons maple syrup

2 teaspoons sherry vinegar

2 teaspoons vegan
  Worcestershire sauce

½ teaspoon liquid smoke

½ teaspoon smoked sea salt, divided

¼ teaspoon freshly ground
  black pepper

FOR THE SANDWICHES

8 slices whole-grain bread

¼ cup vegan mayonnaise

¼ head iceberg lettuce,
  outer leaves removed

2 tomatoes, cut into thin rounds

1 avocado, peeled and sliced

TIP A vegetable peeler will provide the best carrot bacon slices, but if you don't have one and need to cut thin strips with a knife, you'll want to cook the bacon a little longer to achieve the same crisp texture.

First things first, let's talk carrot bacon. Its smoky-sweet crispness makes it the ideal alternative to real bacon in a BLT. And we're from California, so there must always be a few slices of A (avocado) in the equation. Whether you call this sandwich a BLTCA, a TALCB, or a CALBT, everyone will be asking you for the recipe.

TO PREPARE THE CARROT BACON

1. Preheat oven to 400°F.

2. Line a baking sheet with parchment paper.

3. Over a big bowl, use a vegetable peeler to peel carrots into thin strips. Add oil, maple syrup, vinegar, Worcestershire sauce, liquid smoke, ¼ teaspoon smoked sea salt, and pepper and toss to coat. Spread out carrots and marinating liquid on baking sheet.

4. Bake for 18 to 21 minutes, flipping occasionally. Once out of the oven, toss with remaining ¼ teaspoon smoked sea salt.

TO PREPARE THE SANDWICHES

1. Toast bread in toaster oven until golden.

2. Spread 4 slices bread with mayonnaise. Top with lettuce, tomato, avocado, and a few pieces bacon. Top with remaining bread and serve.

Tempeh Reuben Sandwich with Russian Dressing

NUT-FREE • **30 MINUTES OR LESS**

Makes 4 sandwiches

Prep time: 10 minutes

Cook time: 15 minutes

FOR THE TEMPEH

1 (8-ounce) package tempeh, cut into ¼-inch-thick strips

½ red beet, peeled and grated

2 tablespoons freshly squeezed lemon juice

1 tablespoon stone-ground mustard

1 tablespoon brown rice syrup

¼ teaspoon sea salt

¼ teaspoon freshly ground black pepper

¼ teaspoon red pepper flakes

½ teaspoon caraway seeds

2 teaspoons neutral-tasting oil

FOR THE DRESSING

3 tablespoons vegan mayonnaise

2 tablespoons ketchup

1 teaspoon brown rice syrup

1 tablespoon fresh chives, finely chopped

¼ teaspoon sea salt

¼ teaspoon freshly ground black pepper

FOR THE SANDWICHES

2 teaspoons neutral-tasting oil

8 slices rye bread

4 slices vegan mozzarella or provolone cheese

⅓ cup sauerkraut

The essence of a Reuben comes from the combo of toasted rye bread (preferably marble rye), sauerkraut, and cheese. Throw some tasty tempeh in the middle of this wondrous trifecta, seal the deal with vegan Russian dressing, and you'll forget there ever was a meat version.

TO PREPARE THE TEMPEH

1. Fill a pot with about 1 inch of water and place a steamer basket in pot. Bring to a simmer with a lid on. Steam tempeh for 5 to 7 minutes. Set aside to cool slightly.

2. In a large bowl, combine tempeh, beet, lemon juice, mustard, brown rice syrup, sea salt, black pepper, red pepper flakes, and caraway seeds. Stir to combine. Heat a medium sauté pan over medium heat and add oil. Sauté tempeh mixture for 5 to 7 minutes, or until slightly golden. Set aside.

TO PREPARE THE DRESSING

In a small bowl, whisk all dressing ingredients until uniform. Set aside.

TO PREPARE THE SANDWICHES

Heat a griddle and add oil. Add 4 slices bread to griddle. Top with 2 teaspoons dressing, 2 slices tempeh and beet mixture, 1 slice cheese, and 1 tablespoon sauerkraut. Top with remaining bread slices, flip, and cook on second side until golden, about 2 to 3 minutes. Serve warm.

TIP If you don't have time to cook your own tempeh, try this recipe with vegan deli meat. We prefer smoked Tofurky slices for this sandwich.

Hearts of Palm Mozzarella Sticks

30 MINUTES OR LESS

Makes 20 pieces

Prep time: 8 minutes

Cook time: 10 minutes

2 tablespoons unbleached
all-purpose flour

10 stalks hearts of palm, halved
lengthwise (2 to 3 jars or cans)

½ cup unsweetened almond milk

1 tablespoon freshly squeezed
lemon juice

2 teaspoons brown rice syrup

⅓ cup whole-wheat bread crumbs

2 tablespoons vegan Parmesan

½ teaspoon dried oregano

¼ teaspoon dried basil

¼ teaspoon garlic powder

¼ teaspoon sea salt

¼ teaspoon freshly ground
black pepper

1 to 2 tablespoons neutral-tasting oil

2 cups jarred marinara sauce

When we went vegan many years ago, we found ourselves missing mozzarella sticks. So we started experimenting to come up with the solution to this very serious problem. It turns out that hearts of palm make a wonderful mozzarella substitute. They have the color, texture, and flavor you want in a mozzie stick.

1. Place flour in a shallow bowl or plate. Add hearts of palm and coat. Set aside.

2. In a mixing bowl, combine almond milk, lemon juice, and brown rice syrup. Whisk until uniform. Add hearts of palm and submerge.

3. In a separate large bowl, combine bread crumbs, Parmesan, oregano, basil, garlic powder, sea salt, and pepper. Whisk until uniform.

4. Heat a medium sauté pan over medium heat and add oil.

5. Dredge each piece of hearts of palm in bread crumb mixture and place in pan. Sauté for 5 to 7 minutes, or until golden, flipping occasionally.

6. While mozzarella sticks are cooking, heat marinara sauce in small pot over medium heat until warm. Serve mozzarella sticks with marinara sauce, for dipping.

TIP When buying hearts of palm, look for jars or cans that say "sustainably harvested." This label indicates that the base plant has lots of branches that can be harvested one at a time, allowing other branches, and the tree itself, to keep growing.

White Pizza with Shaved Carrots and Olive Gremolata

NUT-FREE

Makes 1 (12-inch) pizza

Prep time: 20 minutes

Cook time: 22 to 24 minutes

FOR THE WHITE SAUCE

1 tablespoon vegan butter

1 shallot, finely chopped

2 cloves garlic, finely chopped

1 tablespoon unbleached all-purpose flour

½ cup soy milk creamer

¼ teaspoon dried oregano

¼ teaspoon sea salt

¼ teaspoon freshly ground black pepper

1 teaspoon white wine vinegar

FOR THE GREMOLATA

¼ cup packed fresh parsley

2 tablespoons extra-virgin olive oil

1 clove garlic, coarsely chopped

1 tablespoon freshly squeezed lemon juice, plus zest of ½ lemon

¼ teaspoon red pepper flakes

⅛ teaspoon sea salt

2 tablespoons Kalamata olives, coarsely chopped

1 premade pizza dough

1 carrot, shaved with vegetable peeler

Gremolata can be described as fancy Italian parsley pesto. Pairing it with the more pedestrian pizza turns "an end of the week and I'm tired" dinner into a sophisticated pie, perfect for those nights when you want quotidian with a side of pizzazz.

Preheat oven to 450°F. If using pizza stone, heat with oven.

TO PREPARE THE WHITE SAUCE

Heat a saucepan over medium heat and add butter, shallot, and garlic. Cook about 3 minutes until softened. Whisk in flour. Add creamer, oregano, sea salt, pepper, and vinegar, and whisk. Cook for 5 to 7 minutes, or until sauce is thick and creamy. Set aside.

TO PREPARE THE GREMOLATA

In a food processor, combine parsley, oil, garlic, lemon juice and zest, red pepper flakes, and sea salt. Pulse until uniform. Fold in olives.

TO PREPARE THE PIZZA

1. On a floured surface shape pizza dough into a 12-inch round. Top with white sauce, carrot, and gremolata.

2. Bake for 22 to 24 minutes, or until bubbles appear in center of pizza. Serve warm.

TIP Many grocery stores offer premade pizza dough that you can roll out and stretch to your desired thickness. Typically, the texture more closely resembles a freshly made pizza than a prefabricated crust does.

Personal Baked Nacho Cups

NUT-FREE · 30 MINUTES OR LESS

Makes 12 cups
Prep time: 5 minutes
Cook time: 22 minutes

4 to 6 flour tortillas
2 teaspoons neutral-tasting oil
½ teaspoon sea salt
¼ teaspoon freshly ground
   black pepper
¼ teaspoon garlic powder
¼ teaspoon smoked paprika
1 teaspoon freshly squeezed lime juice
1 cup shredded vegan cheese
½ red bell pepper, finely diced
2 scallions, cut into thin rounds
¼ cup vegan sour cream
1 small fresh jalapeño, seeded
   and cut into thin rounds

When you and your friends order nachos, everyone ends up jockeying for chips to get that perfect nacho-to-topping ratio in each bite. We've come up with a solution: personal-size nacho bliss, with all the goodies in a compact crunchy chip cup. The mess and stress of sharing is nacho problem anymore.

1. Preheat oven to 375°F.

2. Cut each tortilla into 4 wedges. Spray a muffin pan with oil and gently press tortilla wedges into each cup to fill all 12 cups. Brush lightly with oil and sprinkle with sea salt, pepper, garlic powder, and paprika. Drizzle with lime juice.

3. Bake for 12 to 14 minutes, or until golden. Remove from oven.

4. Add 1 to 2 tablespoons cheese and evenly disperse red bell pepper to each cup.

5. Return pan to oven and bake for 6 to 8 minutes, or until cups are crunchy and cheese is melted.

6. Remove from heat and add scallions, sour cream, and 1 slice jalapeño to each cup. Serve warm.

TIP Make this dish into a mini taco salad by adding shredded lettuce to each cup.

Recipe p.156

6

Mains

Did you know that kale and mushrooms have protein? And cauliflower, acorn squash, and bok choy all have omega-3 fatty acids? When thinking about how to cook like a vegan, it helps to shift your mind-set and see your dinner plate in a whole new way. Many of the dishes we create have a nutritious, satisfying blend of carbs, protein, and veggies, combined in ways you might not expect.

Whether you're new to cooking in general or an old hand, we encourage you to read the recipe the whole way through before getting out your knife and cutting board. Once you get a good grasp of the general way a vegan recipe unfolds, putting the meal together is as easy as 1-2-3.

Greek Lentils with Olives and Herbs

GLUTEN-FREE

Serves 4 to 6

Prep time: 12 minutes

Cook time: 25 minutes

FOR THE LENTILS

1 cup dried green lentils

2 cloves garlic, slightly crushed

1 teaspoon dried thyme

1 bay leaf

FOR THE DRESSING

3 tablespoons freshly squeezed lemon juice, plus zest of 1 lemon

2 tablespoons extra-virgin olive oil

1 tablespoon brown rice syrup

2 teaspoons fresh oregano, stemmed and finely chopped

½ teaspoon sea salt

¼ teaspoon freshly ground black pepper

FOR THE ADD-INS

½ cup cherry tomatoes, quartered

⅓ cup Kalamata olives, sliced

2 tablespoons fresh chives, finely chopped

1 Persian (or ½ English) cucumber, diced

Sea salt

Freshly ground black pepper

2 tablespoons toasted pine nuts

Lentils are perfection, but you probably already knew that. In case you didn't, here are a few reasons why: They're high in protein and fiber, cook up in about 15 minutes, and blend well with flavors from Greece and Italy to Asia and beyond. It doesn't hurt that they're also inexpensive. Eat them warm or cold, on their own or as a side dish, now or later, and you can't go wrong.

TO PREPARE THE LENTILS

Fill a 6-quart pot halfway with salted water and bring to a boil. Add lentils, garlic, thyme, and bay leaf and return to boil, then lower to a simmer. Cook for 15 to 20 minutes, or until lentils are tender. Drain lentils and discard bay leaf.

TO PREPARE THE DRESSING

Whisk together lemon juice and zest, oil, brown rice syrup, oregano, sea salt, and pepper in a small bowl and set aside.

Place cooked lentils in a large serving bowl. Coat with dressing and add tomatoes, olives, chives, and cucumbers. Season with sea salt and pepper to taste. Serve warm or at room temperature, topped with pine nuts.

Variations

If you love lentils as much as we do, you know there's no reason to limit yourself to just one color of these nutritious gems. Try red lentils in the Sloppy Joe variation here, or sub in regular brown lentils for the green in any of these options. Be sure to check the cooking times, since those vary a bit depending on the type of lentil you're using.

Warm Lentil Salad with Figs and Pistachios

½ cup toasted pistachios, coarsely chopped
20 dried figs, coarsely chopped
1 small carrot, finely chopped
½ English cucumber, finely diced
½ cup vegan ricotta, crumbled
Sea salt
Freshly ground black pepper

1. Cook lentils as written in original recipe.

2. Make dressing as written in original recipe, but omit oregano. Coat lentils with dressing, and combine with substitute add-ins. Season with sea salt and pepper to taste.

Sloppy Joe Lentils with Spinach

1 tablespoon neutral-tasting oil
½ yellow onion, finely chopped
2 cloves garlic, finely chopped
6 ounces vegan meat crumbles
1 tablespoon vegan Worcestershire sauce
2 tablespoons freshly squeezed lemon juice
2 cups packed baby spinach
1 cup jarred pizza sauce or marinara sauce
Vegan hamburger buns (optional), for serving

1. Cook lentils as written in original recipe.
2. While lentils are cooking, heat a medium sauté pan over medium heat and add oil. Add onion, garlic, meat crumbles, Worcestershire sauce, and lemon juice and cook for about 5 minutes, or until onions are soft. Add spinach and cook about 2 minutes, or until wilted. Add pizza sauce and stir constantly until warmed, about 1 minute.
3. Place cooked, drained lentils in bowl and add onion-meat mixture. Serve warm in hamburger buns, or alone as a main dish.

Ginger and Shiitake Lentils

1 tablespoon neutral-tasting oil
1 shallot, finely chopped
10 shiitake mushrooms, stemmed
  and cut into thin strips
1 large carrot, diced
¼ cup scallions, thinly sliced
1 tablespoon fresh ginger, finely grated
2 tablespoons rice vinegar
2 tablespoons tamari
1 tablespoon hot pepper sesame oil

1. Cook lentils as written in original recipe.
2. While lentils are cooking, heat a medium sauté pan over medium heat and add neutral-tasting oil. Add shallot, mushrooms, and carrot and cook for about 5 minutes, or until onions are soft and mushrooms have released liquid.
3. Place cooked, drained lentils in bowl and add cooked mushroom mixture, scallions, ginger, vinegar, tamari, and sesame oil. Toss to combine and serve warm.

Black Bean Fritters with Macadamia-Basil Topping

Makes 12 large or
24 small patties

Prep time: 15 minutes,
plus 10 minutes to rest

Cook time: 10 minutes

If you want to experiment with the fun-loving, popular cousin of croquettes and burger patties, make some fritters. Serve them as a main dish or appetizer, or even top a salad with them and they'll fit in anywhere and make friends with everyone.

FOR THE FRITTERS

2 (16-ounce) cans black beans, rinsed and drained

½ teaspoon sea salt

2 tablespoons freshly squeezed lemon juice

2 tablespoons red wine vinegar

1 tablespoon agave

¾ cup unbleached all-purpose flour

¼ cup finely ground yellow cornmeal

1 red bell pepper, finely diced

¼ yellow onion, finely diced

1 bunch fresh chives, finely chopped

2 tablespoons neutral-tasting oil

FOR THE TOPPING

½ cup toasted macadamia nuts, coarsely chopped

8 to 10 fresh basil leaves, finely chopped

½ teaspoon freshly squeezed lemon juice

⅛ teaspoon sea salt

TO PREPARE THE FRITTERS

1. In a food processor or blender, combine black beans, sea salt, lemon juice, vinegar, and agave. Pulse about 10 times. Add flour and cornmeal and pulse until mixture holds together.

2. Transfer mixture to a large bowl and fold in bell pepper, onion, and chives. Incorporate until uniform. Allow mixture to rest for 10 minutes to allow liquids to absorb into flour.

3. Heat a large skillet over medium heat and add oil. With damp hands, form mixture into small patties and cook about 5 minutes on each side, or until patties are browned and crisp around edges.

TO PREPARE THE TOPPING

In a bowl, combine macadamia nuts, basil, lemon juice, and sea salt.

Serve warm patties topped with about 1 teaspoon of macadamia-basil topping.

TIP Use an ice cream scoop to make fritters that are all the same size. This trick can be used for uniform patties, cookies, and more.

Brazil Nut Pesto-Stuffed Mushrooms

GLUTEN-FREE

30 MINUTES OR LESS

Serves 4 to 6

Prep time: 15 minutes

Cook time: 13 minutes

FOR THE MUSHROOMS

12 to 16 cremini mushrooms, or 6 large portobellos

2 tablespoons extra-virgin olive oil

2 tablespoons red wine vinegar

1 teaspoon maple syrup

½ teaspoon sea salt

½ teaspoon freshly ground black pepper

FOR THE PESTO

1 bulb garlic, top sliced off to expose cloves

1¼ teaspoons neutral-tasting oil, divided

¼ cup extra-virgin olive oil

2 tablespoons freshly squeezed lemon juice

1½ cups packed fresh basil leaves

½ cup toasted Brazil nuts

1 teaspoon light miso paste

¼ teaspoon sea salt

¼ teaspoon freshly ground black pepper

TIP Mushrooms release liquid when cooked. Be sure to cook them until all the liquid evaporates and let them rest for a few minutes before serving, so they retain their shape.

In a nut-wrestling match, Brazil nuts would always come out the victor. They're not only hearty, but they're also packed with nutrients including selenium, a potent anticancer, antibacterial, and anti-aging antioxidant. That's a lot of anti rolled into one pro nut. When stuffed into mushrooms they make a meal that everyone will enjoy without feeling like they're eating "health" food.

Preheat oven to 375°F.

TO PREPARE THE MUSHROOMS

In a large shallow dish, combine mushrooms, oil, vinegar, maple syrup, sea salt, and pepper and coat well. Set aside to marinate.

TO PREPARE THE PESTO

1. Roast garlic: place garlic cut-side down in heatproof ramekin. Drizzle garlic with ¼ teaspoon neutral-tasting oil. Roast for 35 minutes until cloves are soft.

2. When cool enough to handle, remove 4 cloves roasted garlic from the bulb and use the blade of a knife to squeeze flesh out of skin into food processor. Add olive oil and lemon juice and blend for a few seconds. Add basil, Brazil nuts, miso, sea salt, and pepper and pulse until uniform and smooth.

Heat a large sauté pan over medium heat and add remaining 1 teaspoon neutral-tasting oil. Add mushrooms and marinating liquid and cook cap-side down for 3 to 4 minutes. Flip and fill each cremini mushroom with 1 to 2 tablespoons pesto mixture or ¼ cup pesto for large portobellos. Cook for a further 7 to 9 minutes, or until mushrooms are soft. Serve warm.

White Bean Provençal Stuffed Zucchini

NUT-FREE

Serves 4 to 6

Prep time: 10 minutes,
plus 20 minutes to marinate

Cook time: 20 minutes

FOR THE ZUCCHINI

4 medium zucchini

2 teaspoons maple syrup

2 teaspoons extra-virgin olive oil

2 teaspoons sherry vinegar or
  red wine vinegar

¼ teaspoon sea salt

¼ teaspoon freshly ground
  black pepper

The south of France is known for its beauty and abundance of produce and herbs such as thyme, rosemary, sage, and savory. We wrap up these flavors into a one-dish dinner that will spice up your weekly repertoire.

Preheat oven to 425°F.

TO PREPARE THE ZUCCHINI

1. Slice zucchini in half lengthwise. Hollow out zucchini by removing inner, seeded portion with melon baller or spoon, keeping ends intact and creating a boat.

2. In a small mixing bowl, whisk maple syrup, oil, vinegar, sea salt, and pepper.

3. Lay zucchini in a baking dish, hollow-side up. Drizzle with maple syrup mixture and set aside for 10 to 20 minutes to marinate.

FOR THE FILLING

3 slices spelt or whole-wheat bread

2 teaspoons extra-virgin olive oil

1 teaspoon maple syrup

1 teaspoon sherry vinegar or
red wine vinegar

1 tablespoon fresh rosemary, stemmed
and finely chopped

½ teaspoon herbes de Provence

¼ teaspoon sea salt

¼ teaspoon freshly ground
black pepper

1 (16-ounce) can white beans
(navy or cannellini), rinsed
and drained

2 teaspoons neutral-tasting oil

TO PREPARE THE FILLING

In a food processor, combine bread, olive oil, maple syrup, vinegar, rosemary, herbes de Provence, sea salt, and pepper and pulse until bread crumb consistency is reached. Place in bowl and fold in white beans.

TO COOK THE STUFFED ZUCCHINI

1. Heat a large ovenproof skillet over medium heat and add neutral-tasting oil.

2. Add 3 tablespoons bread crumb mixture to each zucchini boat, filling to the top and spreading evenly. Place stuffed zucchini in the skillet, filled-side up.

3. Cook over medium-low heat for 8 to 10 minutes, then transfer skillet to oven. Bake for about 10 minutes, or until filling is golden. Serve warm.

TIP If you have a melon baller, now's the time to bust it out. It's the perfect tool for hollowing out your zucchini. What to do with the leftover zucchini filling? Throw it into a stir-fry or pasta later in the week.

Yellow Thai Coconut Curry

GLUTEN-FREE • **NUT-FREE**

Serves 4 to 6

Prep time: 15 minutes

Cook time: 18 minutes

1 cup water

1 medium russet potato, peeled and diced

2 carrots, cut into thin rounds

2 tablespoons virgin coconut oil

1 shallot, finely chopped

1 (12-ounce) container extra-firm tofu, drained, pressed, and diced

2 tablespoons yellow curry powder

1 baby bok choy, coarsely chopped

1 cup frozen green peas

2 (13.5-ounce) cans full-fat coconut milk

⅓ cup freshly squeezed lime juice, plus zest of 1 lime

2 tablespoons tamari

1 tablespoon rice vinegar

1 tablespoon evaporated cane sugar

½ teaspoon sea salt

2 cups cooked white or brown rice (optional)

Let's combine cooking and geography class for a moment. Take a map of the world and note where curry is popular. Most of the globe, right? From Indonesia to Japan, Thailand to India, and even the Caribbean, curry is as ubiquitous as the rice it's typically served with. This yellow curry is our take on the Thai version. And there's a reason curry rhymes with hurry, because you can make this in a snap.

1. In a large sauté pan with a lid, add water. Cover and heat over medium heat. Once simmering, add potato, cover, and steam about 3 minutes.

2. Add carrots, cover, and steam for about 2 more minutes. Drain excess water, leaving potato and carrots in pan.

3. Add oil, shallot, tofu, and curry powder and sauté for about 3 minutes.

4. Add bok choy, peas, coconut milk, lime juice and zest, tamari, vinegar, sugar, and sea salt and stir to incorporate. Reduce heat to medium-low and cook until vegetables are soft and the mixture is bright yellow, about 10 minutes.

5. Serve hot over cooked rice (if using).

TIP This curry grows in flavor and color over time. It holds well for up to 3 days in the refrigerator.

Lucky Black-Eyed Pea Croquettes

NUT-FREE • 30 MINUTES OR LESS

Makes 6 or 8 large croquettes

Prep time: 15 minutes

Cook time: 15 minutes

FOR THE CROQUETTES

2 tablespoons neutral-tasting oil, plus 1 teaspoon, divided

1 small zucchini, finely chopped

½ yellow onion, finely chopped

½ red bell pepper, finely chopped

1 (15-ounce) can black-eyed peas, rinsed and drained

2 or 3 cloves roasted garlic (see Tip)

½ teaspoon sea salt

½ teaspoon freshly ground black pepper

½ teaspoon dried rosemary

2 tablespoons freshly squeezed lemon juice

2 tablespoons vegan Worcestershire sauce

1 tablespoon brown rice syrup

½ cup yellow cornmeal

½ cup rolled oats

1 tablespoon fresh sage (5 to 7 leaves), finely chopped

½ cup bread crumbs

For centuries, people around the world have eaten black-eyed peas to bring good luck and prosperity in the New Year. A popular ingredient in the American South, this bean (yes!) is traditionally cooked with animal ingredients, but once you try our version, you'll see you don't necessarily need meat products to enjoy this flavorful and delicious legume. So eat up and get lucky!

TO PREPARE THE CROQUETTES

1. Heat a medium sauté pan over medium heat. Add 1 teaspoon oil. Add zucchini, onion, and bell pepper and cook 3 to 5 minutes, or until softened.

2. In a food processor, combine black-eyed peas, roasted garlic, sea salt, pepper, rosemary, lemon juice, Worcestershire sauce, and brown rice syrup. Pulse 5 to 10 times. Add cornmeal and oats, and pulse until mixture holds together. Fold in sage.

3. Transfer black-eyed pea mixture to a large bowl and add cooked vegetables. Incorporate until uniform.

4. Heat a large skillet over medium heat and add remaining 2 tablespoons oil. Place bread crumbs in shallow bowl. With damp hands, form mixture into football shape and coat in bread crumbs. Gently shake off excess crumbs and place in skillet. Cook for 3 to 5 minutes on each side, or until browned.

FOR THE SHALLOTS

1 tablespoon neutral-tasting oil

3 or 4 shallots, cut into thin strips

¼ teaspoon sea salt

¼ teaspoon freshly ground
  black pepper

½ teaspoon maple syrup

½ teaspoon freshly squeezed
  lemon juice

TO PREPARE THE SHALLOTS

Heat a small sauté pan over medium heat and add oil. Add shallots, sea salt, and pepper. Cook 3 to 5 minutes, or until crisp. Stir in maple syrup and lemon juice.

Serve croquettes warm, topped with shallots.

TIP See page 72 for instructions on how to roast garlic.

TIP Besides being a bean and not a pea, black-eyed peas are packed with vitamin K, which helps blood to clot when needed.

Southern BBQ Jackfruit Cabbage Cups

GLUTEN-FREE
Serves 4 to 6
Prep time: 15 minutes
Cook time: 20 minutes

Jackfruit is the new go-to of any vegan chuckwagon. This buckaroo effortlessly transforms into pulled pork, burgers, and more, all with few calories and no fat. It loves moseying into barbecue sauce, soaking up the sweet, smoky, rich flavors.

FOR THE BBQ SAUCE

2 teaspoons neutral-tasting oil
2 cloves garlic, finely chopped
1 yellow onion, finely chopped, divided
1 cup ketchup
¼ cup orange juice
3 tablespoons apple cider vinegar
3 tablespoons brown rice syrup
2 tablespoons molasses
1 tablespoon vegan
    Worcestershire sauce
2 tablespoons evaporated cane sugar
1 teaspoon dried mustard
½ teaspoon sea salt
¼ teaspoon freshly ground
    black pepper
¼ teaspoon cayenne pepper
¼ teaspoon ground cinnamon

FOR THE JACKFRUIT

2 (19-ounce) cans young jackfruit,
    rinsed and drained
2 teaspoons neutral-tasting oil
⅛ teaspoon sea salt
⅛ teaspoon freshly ground
    black pepper
½ head red cabbage
¼ cup toasted peanuts, for topping

TO PREPARE THE BBQ SAUCE

Heat a 4-quart saucepan over medium heat, add oil, garlic, and half of the chopped onion (reserve remaining onion for the jackfruit) and cook about 3 minutes, or until softened. Reduce heat to medium-low and add remaining sauce ingredients. Cook for about 5 minutes, stirring occasionally.

TO PREPARE THE JACKFRUIT

1. Break jackfruit apart slightly with hands, and cut base of each piece of jackfruit into small dice. Set aside.

2. Heat oil in a large sauté pan over medium heat and add remaining onion. Sauté for about 3 minutes, or until softened. Add jackfruit to pan and sprinkle with sea salt and pepper. Cook for about 4 minutes, or until browned slightly. Add to pan containing BBQ sauce.

3. Cook for 5 minutes over medium-low heat, stirring carefully, until jackfruit is soft and some sauce is absorbed. Cover pan with splatter screen to prevent sauce from splashing out of pan.

4. Cut out cabbage core and break apart leaves to get cup shapes. Scoop warm jackfruit mixture into cabbage cups and top with peanuts.

TIP Purchase jackfruit online, or at a local Asian market. Be sure to get unripe, or young jackfruit, not mature fruit canned in syrup.

Coconut-Crusted Oyster Mushrooms with Cocktail Sauce

NUT-FREE • 30 MINUTES OR LESS

Makes 12 to 14 pieces

Prep time: 10 minutes

Cook time: 8 minutes

FOR THE MUSHROOMS

½ cup panko bread crumbs

½ cup unsweetened coconut flakes, finely shredded

¼ cup unbleached all-purpose flour

½ teaspoon sea salt

¼ teaspoon freshly ground black pepper

¼ teaspoon cayenne pepper

¼ teaspoon garlic powder

1 teaspoon evaporated cane sugar

⅓ cup Ener-G Egg Replacer

¾ cup water

¼ teaspoon kelp granules

12 to 14 fresh oyster mushrooms

2 tablespoons neutral-tasting oil

FOR THE COCKTAIL SAUCE

⅔ cup ketchup

2 teaspoons freshly squeezed lemon juice

2 teaspoons brown rice syrup

2 teaspoons vegan Worcestershire sauce

1 teaspoon hot sauce

2 teaspoons horseradish, finely grated

¼ teaspoon sea salt

¼ teaspoon freshly ground black pepper

There's nothing shrimpy about plump, luscious oyster mushrooms. They are terrific sources of minerals like zinc and potassium. If you know anyone who's on the fence about mushrooms, cook this recipe for them. Battered meaty mushrooms with a tangy dipping sauce—what's not to like?

TO PREPARE THE MUSHROOMS

1. In a large bowl, whisk together panko bread crumbs, coconut flakes, flour, sea salt, pepper, cayenne, garlic powder, and sugar. Set aside.

2. In a large bowl, vigorously whisk egg replacer and water for about 2 minutes, or until mixture is thick and foamy. Add kelp granules and whisk. Dip mushrooms, one at a time, submerging completely, then removing and gently shaking off excess egg replacer mixture. Dredge mushrooms in panko-coconut mixture.

3. Heat a large sauté pan over medium-high heat and add oil. Carefully add mushrooms and cook 4 to 5 minutes, or until golden. Turn mushrooms over and cook about 3 additional minutes, or until golden.

TO PREPARE THE COCKTAIL SAUCE

In a mixing bowl, whisk together all sauce ingredients. Set aside to develop flavors, about 10 to 30 minutes.

Serve mushrooms warm, with cocktail sauce on the side.

TIP Kelp granules are dried powdered sea veggies. They add just a hint of that "oceany" essence you're looking for with veganized seafood dishes.

Acorn Squash Fritters with Korean Spicy Sauce

NUT-FREE

Makes about 8 (3-inch) fritters
Prep time: 10 minutes
Cook time: 45 minutes

Drizzle Korean spicy sauce on pretty much anything, and you'll wind up with a hit. Combined with these crispy-on-the-outside, smooth-in-the-middle fritters, you're likely to have anyone who tastes them clamoring for more. Our advice? Make a double batch.

FOR THE FRITTERS

1 acorn squash, halved and seeded
1 teaspoon neutral-tasting oil, plus 2 tablespoons, divided
1½ cups panko bread crumbs, plus ½ cup, divided
½ cup unbleached all-purpose flour
1 tablespoon rice vinegar
2 teaspoons tamari
2 teaspoons brown rice syrup
2 teaspoons toasted sesame oil
½ teaspoon sea salt
2 teaspoons fresh ginger, finely grated
2 teaspoons black sesame seeds
1 tablespoon scallions, thinly sliced

FOR THE SAUCE

⅓ cup vegan gochujang sauce
2 teaspoons rice vinegar
1 tablespoon brown rice syrup
1 teaspoon freshly squeezed lime juice
1 teaspoon toasted sesame oil
1 teaspoon black sesame seeds

TIP Gochujang is the Korean equivalent of ketchup, because it pairs well with so many dishes, but it does pack a punch. In this recipe, we spruce it up with vinegar and lime.

TO PREPARE THE FRITTERS

1. Preheat oven to 400°F. Place squash cut-side up on a baking sheet and drizzle each half with 1 teaspoon neutral-tasting oil. Roast for 36 to 38 minutes, or until knife easily pierces flesh. Set aside to cool.

2. Scoop out 2½ cups squash flesh and place in large bowl. Mash with potato masher. Add 1½ cups panko, flour, vinegar, tamari, brown rice syrup, sesame oil, sea salt, and ginger. Whisk. Fold in sesame seeds and scallions.

3. In a shallow bowl, place remaining ½ cup panko. Scoop ⅓ cup squash mixture and roll in panko. Flatten into a 3-inch disk. Repeat with remaining squash mixture.

4. Heat a large nonstick sauté pan and add 2 tablespoons oil. Add fritters and cook about 4 minutes per side, or until golden.

TO PREPARE THE SAUCE

In a mixing bowl combine gochujang sauce, vinegar, brown rice syrup, lime juice, oil, and sesame seeds. Whisk until uniform.

Serve fritters warm, drizzled with sauce.

Chicken Fillets over Spinach Citrus Cream

Makes 8 fillets
Prep time: 15 minutes
Cook time: 43 minutes

This dish has a whole lotta wow and a little citrus pow. The vegan chicken fillets add a meaty consistency and are great for a satisfying meal without a lot of prep time. The spinach cream helps you get your daily greens without having to chew your way through a giant salad.

FOR THE ROASTED GARLIC

1 bulb garlic, top sliced off to expose cloves
¼ teaspoon neutral-tasting oil
Pinch sea salt
Pinch freshly ground black pepper

FOR THE FILLETS

8 vegan chicken fillets
2 tablespoons freshly squeezed lemon juice
1 tablespoon brown rice syrup
2 teaspoons red wine vinegar
½ teaspoon sea salt, divided
½ teaspoon freshly ground black pepper, divided
½ cup whole-wheat bread crumbs
½ teaspoon dried basil
½ teaspoon dried oregano
1 tablespoon neutral-tasting oil

Preheat oven to 375°F.

TO ROAST THE GARLIC

Place garlic bulb cut-side down in a heatproof ramekin and drizzle with oil, pinch sea salt, and pinch pepper. Roast for about 35 minutes, or until cloves are soft.

TO PREPARE THE FILLETS

1. Place chicken in a baking dish. In a small bowl, whisk lemon juice, brown rice syrup, vinegar, ¼ teaspoon sea salt, and ¼ teaspoon pepper. Drizzle over chicken. Set aside.

2. In a shallow dish, mix together bread crumbs, basil, oregano, remaining ¼ teaspoon sea salt, and remaining ¼ teaspoon pepper. Gently dredge each piece of chicken in bread crumb mixture. Shake off any excess crumbs.

3. Heat a large sauté pan over medium-high heat and add oil. Cook on each side for about 4 minutes, or until browned and crisp.

FOR THE SPINACH CREAM

2 cups tightly packed fresh
    baby spinach

¼ cup toasted cashews

¼ cup toasted walnuts

3 tablespoons extra-virgin olive oil

2 tablespoons freshly squeezed
    grapefruit juice, plus zest of
    ½ grapefruit

2 tablespoons freshly squeezed
    lemon juice, plus zest of ½ lemon

2 teaspoons light miso paste

¼ teaspoon sea salt

¼ teaspoon freshly ground
    black pepper

TO PREPARE THE SPINACH CREAM

Remove 4 cloves roasted garlic from bulb and use blade of a knife to squeeze flesh out of skin into a high-powered blender or food processor. Add spinach, cashews, walnuts, oil, grapefruit juice and zest, lemon juice and zest, miso, sea salt, and pepper. Blend for about 30 seconds, or until smooth.

Serve warm fillets over spinach cream.

TIP We recommend Gardein brand Scallopini for vegan fillets, if you can find them in your local grocer. If you are unable to find them or an equivalent chicken substitute, you can always substitute drained and pressed extra-firm tofu, cut into ¼-inch-thick strips.

Hearts of Palm Tofu Crab Cakes with Spicy Rémoulade

30 MINUTES OR LESS

Makes 10 (3-inch) round cakes

Prep time: 12 minutes

Cook time: 8 minutes

FOR THE RÉMOULADE

2 tablespoons vegan sour cream

1 tablespoon vegan mayonnaise

2 teaspoons hot sauce

1 teaspoon freshly squeezed lemon juice, plus zest of ½ lemon

1 teaspoon brown rice syrup

¼ teaspoon sea salt

¼ teaspoon freshly ground black pepper

FOR THE COATING

½ cup bread crumbs

1 teaspoon dried mustard

¼ teaspoon cayenne pepper

¼ teaspoon garlic powder

¼ teaspoon sea salt

¼ teaspoon freshly ground black pepper

A New England specialty, crab cakes have become popular worldwide because of their unique flavor—but the secret to this dish is not in the crab, it's in the seasoning! So if you can find Old Bay, you're on your way to crab cake perfection. And when you combine good ol' tofu and hearts of palm—*voilà!*—you get a crab texture that would fool anyone in Baltimore.

TO PREPARE THE RÉMOULADE

In a small bowl, whisk sour cream, mayonnaise, hot sauce, lemon juice and zest, brown rice syrup, sea salt, and pepper. Set aside.

TO PREPARE THE COATING

In a shallow dish, mix bread crumbs, mustard, cayenne, garlic powder, sea salt, and pepper until uniform. Set aside.

FOR THE TOFU

1 (14-ounce) container extra-firm tofu, drained and pressed

3 stalks hearts of palm, diced

½ cup bread crumbs

2 tablespoons fresh parsley (about ¼ bunch), finely chopped

2 tablespoons freshly squeezed lemon juice, plus zest of ½ lemon

1 tablespoon brown rice syrup or agave

3 to 4 tablespoons plus 2 teaspoons neutral-tasting oil, divided

1 teaspoon vegan Worcestershire sauce

1 tablespoon Dijon or German mustard

2 teaspoons Old Bay seasoning or seafood seasoning

½ teaspoon kelp granules

¼ teaspoon sea salt

¼ teaspoon freshly ground black pepper

10 fresh parsley sprigs, for garnish

TO PREPARE THE TOFU

In a large bowl, crumble tofu with hands until uniform. Fold in hearts of palm, bread crumbs, parsley, lemon juice and zest, brown rice syrup or agave, 2 teaspoons oil, Worcestershire sauce, mustard, Old Bay or seafood seasoning, kelp, sea salt, and pepper. Stir until well mixed and mixture holds together.

TO PREPARE THE CRAB CAKES

1. Form tofu mixture into patties and coat each patty in bread crumb mixture. Shake off any excess bread crumbs.

2. Heat a large sauté pan over medium heat and add remaining 3 to 4 tablespoons oil. Add tofu crab cakes and cook on each side for 3 to 4 minutes, or until browned and crisp.

3. Serve cakes warm with a dollop of rémoulade on top. Garnish with parsley.

TIP Rémoulade is a fancy term for a mayo-based topping. We like to add a little heat to our recipe, but if you prefer to turn down the spice level, omit the cayenne. You can use this topping for anything from baked potato fries to grilled veggies.

Spaghetti Chef

Serves 4 to 6
Prep time: 12 minutes
Cook time: 37 minutes

FOR THE PASTA

Pinch sea salt

1 (16-ounce) package spaghetti
or bucatini

2 tablespoons extra-virgin olive oil

FOR THE SAUCE

2 tablespoons extra-virgin olive oil

1 yellow onion, finely chopped

2 cloves garlic, finely chopped

½ cup raw almonds, chopped

½ teaspoon sea salt

¼ teaspoon red pepper flakes

1 (6-ounce) can tomato paste

1 (28-ounce) can diced tomatoes,
drained

2 tablespoons freshly squeezed
lemon juice

¼ cup red wine vinegar

¼ cup evaporated cane sugar

1 tablespoon fresh thyme, stemmed
and coarsely chopped

FOR THE GARLIC OIL

⅓ cup extra-virgin olive oil

3 cloves garlic, thinly sliced

TIP Bucatini, a thicker, hollow relative
of spaghetti, works beautifully in this
recipe, so if you can find it, give it a whirl.

Walking down a cobblestone street in Sicily, we came upon a tiny, jam-packed restaurant where the special of the day was "Spaghetti Chef." With no further explanation, except the revelation that it was vegan, we patiently drank wine and waited until 11:30 p.m. for a table. And was it ever worth it! We adapted this dish as an ode to that memorable spot.

TO PREPARE THE PASTA

In a large pot, bring 2 quarts of water to a boil, add sea salt, and cook pasta as directed according to package. Drain pasta and coat with olive oil. Set aside.

TO PREPARE THE SAUCE

1. Heat a high-walled pan over medium-low heat. Add oil, onion, and garlic and cook about 8 minutes, or until caramelized. Add almonds, sea salt, and red pepper flakes and cook 4 more minutes, or until almonds are toasted.

2. Add tomato paste, diced tomatoes, lemon juice, vinegar, and sugar and cook for 20 to 25 minutes, or until sauce is thickened, stirring frequently. Stir in thyme.

TO PREPARE THE GARLIC OIL

In a small saucepan over low heat, cook oil and sliced garlic for about 5 minutes, stirring occasionally, or until fragrant.

To serve, spoon garlic oil into base of pasta serving dish. Add desired amount of pasta over oil and scoop generous helping of thick sauce over pasta. Serve warm.

TIP To further enhance the flavor of the sauce, cook it over a low flame for up to 40 minutes, stirring occasionally.

Down-Home Seitan Fried Chicken

NUT-FREE • 30 MINUTES OR LESS

Serves 4 to 6

Prep time: 5 minutes, plus
10 to 20 minutes to marinate

Cook time: 5 minutes

FOR THE SEITAN

1½ cups soy milk creamer

2 teaspoons apple cider vinegar

2 teaspoons vegan
   Worcestershire sauce

2 (8-ounce) packages seitan
   chunks or strips

⅛ teaspoon sea salt

⅛ teaspoon freshly ground
   black pepper

Fried foods are delicious, and that's why most restaurants have a fryer tucked in their kitchen somewhere. But if you stop and think about what's so appealing, it's the crispiness we all desire. In this recipe, panko bread crumbs deliver the crunch. Take a bite and you'll be transported to a county fair.

TO PREPARE THE SEITAN

In a large bowl, combine creamer and vinegar. Set aside for 2 minutes to curdle. Add Worcestershire sauce. Add seitan pieces and toss to coat. Add sea salt and pepper. Set aside for 10 to 20 minutes.

TIP To test your oil for the perfect cooking temperature, heat it up until you see ripples. Then, stick a clean wooden tool into the oil. If bubbles appear, you're ready to fry.

FOR THE COATING

¾ cup unbleached all-purpose flour

1 teaspoon evaporated cane sugar

¾ teaspoon sea salt, divided

½ teaspoon freshly ground black
  pepper, divided

½ teaspoon dried mustard

¼ teaspoon cayenne pepper,
  plus ⅛ teaspoon, divided

¼ teaspoon garlic powder

⅓ cup Ener-G Egg Replacer

1⅓ cups water

1 cup panko bread crumbs

¼ cup neutral-tasting oil

TO PREPARE THE COATING

1. In a large bowl, whisk together flour, sugar,
½ teaspoon sea salt, ¼ teaspoon pepper, mustard,
¼ teaspoon cayenne, and garlic powder. Remove
and reserve ¼ cup flour mixture.

2. In a medium bowl, whisk egg replacer and water
until mixture is foamy.

3. In a small bowl, combine panko, remaining
¼ teaspoon sea salt, remaining ¼ teaspoon pepper,
and remaining ⅛ teaspoon cayenne. Add reserved
¼ cup seasoned flour mixture and whisk until uniform.

TO COOK THE CHICKEN

1. Add oil to a heavy skillet and heat over medium-
high heat.

2. To coat seitan, dredge each piece of seitan in flour
mixture, then dip into egg replacer mixture, and finally
coat in panko mixture. Shake off excess panko.

3. Carefully place coated seitan pieces into hot oil.
Cook for 2 to 3 minutes, or until golden. Turn over and
cook about 2 additional minutes, or until golden. Once
crisp, place pieces on cooling rack over baking sheet.
Serve warm.

Salt and Pepper Tofu with Glazed Shiitake Mushrooms

GLUTEN-FREE · NUT-FREE

Serves 4 to 6

Prep time: 15 minutes,
plus 30 minutes to marinate

Cook time: 10 minutes

FOR THE TOFU

1 (14-ounce) container extra-firm tofu, drained, pressed, and cut into 1-inch cubes

3 tablespoons brown rice vinegar

2 tablespoons maple syrup

¼ teaspoon sea salt, plus pinch

¼ teaspoon freshly ground black pepper, plus pinch

1 tablespoon neutral-tasting oil

⅓ cup arrowroot powder

FOR THE MUSHROOMS

2 teaspoons neutral-tasting oil

4 to 6 fresh large shiitake mushrooms, stemmed and sliced

1 pint cremini mushrooms, sliced

1 tablespoon tamari

1 tablespoon umeboshi plum vinegar

2 teaspoons maple syrup

1 tablespoon fresh ginger, finely grated

TIP During the spice trade, black pepper was used as currency to pay taxes, and helped drive global explorations.

It sounds too easy, right? Salt and pepper—that's it? With a little TLC from arrowroot and high-quality tofu, this dish can be so much more than you'd expect. When you coat tofu with arrowroot, the texture becomes both crunchy and chewy—giving your meal that extra somethin' somethin.'

TO PREPARE THE TOFU

1. Place tofu in a bowl and drizzle with vinegar, maple syrup, sea salt, and pepper. Set aside to marinate for 10 to 30 minutes.

2. Heat a large skillet over medium heat and add oil.

3. In a small bowl, combine arrowroot with pinch sea salt and pepper. Dredge tofu pieces in arrowroot and shake off excess. Place in skillet and cook for 3 to 4 minutes per side, or until golden and crisp on all sides.

TO PREPARE THE MUSHROOMS

Heat a separate skillet over medium heat and add oil. Add shiitake and cremini mushrooms, tamari, vinegar, maple syrup, and ginger. Cook until soft and well glazed, 3 to 5 minutes.

Serve tofu warm, topped with mushrooms.

TIP Umeboshi plum vinegar is actually a by-product of the brining process of umeboshi plums, used often in Japanese cooking. The saltiness of the vinegar is balanced with a fruity tartness. If you'd like to use a substitute, rice vinegar is acceptable.

Wok-Tossed Sesame-Ginger Seitan

NUT-FREE

Serves 4

Prep time: 15 minutes,
plus 10 minutes to marinate

Cook time: 15 minutes

1 (8-ounce) package seitan strips

2 tablespoons freshly squeezed
lime juice

2 tablespoons tamari

2 tablespoons evaporated cane sugar

1 tablespoon fresh ginger,
finely grated

1 tablespoon neutral-tasting oil,
plus 2 teaspoons, divided

1 yellow onion, cut into thin strips

6 to 8 fresh shiitake mushrooms,
stemmed and thinly sliced

1 carrot, thinly sliced

2 cups snow peas, trimmed and diced

1 baby bok choy, cut into thin strips

2 teaspoons toasted sesame oil

2 teaspoons sesame seeds, for garnish

Learn how to wok your wok and talk your talk. This recipe is a great way to begin making authentic Asian-style meals, with marinated seitan and fresh veggies topped with sesame oil and seeds.

1. Cut seitan into thin strips and transfer to a large bowl. Add lime juice, tamari, sugar, ginger, and 2 teaspoons neutral-tasting oil. Toss to coat and set aside for 10 minutes.

2. Heat a large wok or grill pan over medium-high heat and add remaining 1 tablespoon neutral-tasting oil. Add onion, mushrooms, and carrot. Cook until slightly soft, stirring occasionally, about 5 minutes.

3. Add marinated seitan mixture, snow peas, and bok choy and cook until liquid evaporates, about 10 more minutes, stirring occasionally. Remove from heat. Drizzle with sesame oil and sprinkle sesame seeds over top.

TIP Sesame oil becomes carcinogenic when heated to high temperatures, which is why we add it after the dish is cooked. Don't ever let it smoke in the pan.

Ratatouille

GLUTEN-FREE · **NUT-FREE**

Serves 4 to 6

Prep time: 20 minutes

Cook time: 25 to 30 minutes

1 Italian eggplant,
  cut into ¼-inch-thick rounds

1 teaspoon sea salt, divided,
  plus more for eggplant

3 small zucchini, cut into thin rounds

¼ cup neutral-tasting oil

¾ teaspoon freshly ground
  black pepper, divided

1 teaspoon dried basil

1 teaspoon dried oregano

1 tablespoon agave, plus 2 teaspoons

2 tablespoons freshly squeezed
  lemon juice, plus 2 teaspoons

2 tablespoons extra-virgin olive oil

1 orange bell pepper, diced

1 red bell pepper, diced

1 white onion, diced

2 tablespoons red wine

3 to 4 sprigs fresh thyme, stemmed
  and finely chopped, plus more
  for garnish

1 (28-ounce) can roasted diced
  tomatoes, undrained

Ratatouille is as fun to make as it is to say, and while there are a million ways to prepare it, we have our method and we're sticking to it. Our version combines both roasting and sautéing, bringing out the complex flavors of your veggies without spending all day at your stove top.

1. Preheat oven to 400°F.

2. Sprinkle eggplant rounds with sea salt and sweat for about 10 minutes. Rinse off sea salt and pat dry.

3. Place zucchini rounds and eggplant on a rimmed baking sheet. Toss to coat with oil, ½ teaspoon sea salt, ½ teaspoon pepper, basil, oregano, 2 teaspoons agave, and 2 teaspoons lemon juice. Roast for 20 to 25 minutes, or until well cooked.

4. Meanwhile, in a large sauté pan, heat olive oil. Add bell peppers and onion, and cook for about 5 minutes, or until browned. Add wine, remaining 2 tablespoons lemon juice, remaining 1 tablespoon agave, thyme, tomatoes, remaining ½ teaspoon sea salt, and remaining ¼ teaspoon pepper. Cook for 15 to 20 minutes over a low flame, or until vegetables are well cooked.

5. To assemble, remove eggplant and zucchini from oven. Put one-third of eggplant-zucchini mixture in base of a casserole dish and top with half of pepper-onion mixture. Top with another third of eggplant-zucchini mixture and remaining pepper-onion mixture. Top with remaining eggplant-zucchini mixture. Serve warm, garnished with thyme.

TIP When you're picking out your eggplant, look for a few key things. The eggplant should be unblemished and heavy for its size. To test ripeness, gently press your finger against the flesh—if the eggplant regains its shape easily, it's ripe.

Warm Quinoa Bow with Chickpeas, Roasted Beets, and Fresh Dill

GLUTEN-FREE

Serves 4 to 6

Prep time: 10 minutes

Cook time: 1 hour

FOR THE BEETS

2 beets, whole, unpeeled

1 teaspoon neutral-tasting oil

⅛ teaspoon sea salt

FOR THE QUINOA

3 cups water

3 tablespoons extra-virgin olive oil, divided

¾ teaspoon sea salt, divided, plus pinch

1½ cups quinoa

⅛ teaspoon dried red pepper flakes

4 tablespoons freshly squeezed lemon juice, divided, plus zest of ½ lemon

1 tablespoon brown rice syrup

1 tablespoon stone-ground mustard

1 (15 ounce) can garbanzo beans (chickpeas), rinsed and drained

⅓ cup toasted almonds, coarsely chopped

½ cup fresh dill, finely chopped

TIP Dill is a powerhouse of healing—and it tastes good. It's a natural antibacterial, and it may help neutralize carcinogens.

We know you like quinoa, because who doesn't? You can elevate the flavor of this popular seed by dry roasting before you cook it. Trust us, this isn't your super-hippie quinoa bowl. It's got mad flavor with the combo of crunchy chickpeas, beets, and fresh dill.

Preheat oven to 375°F.

TO PREPARE THE BEETS

Place beets in a small roasting dish. Coat in oil and sprinkle with sea salt. Roast for 45 minutes to 1 hour, or until a knife pierces the flesh easily and skin appears wrinkled. Remove from oven and cover with aluminum foil to steam. This helps separate skin from beet. Set aside until cool enough to peel. Reduce oven heat to 350°F.

TO PREPARE THE QUINOA

1. In a medium saucepan, add water and bring to a boil. Add 1 teaspoon olive oil and ¼ teaspoon sea salt. In a separate medium sauté pan, dry roast quinoa, stirring, until fragrant, about 3 minutes. Add to boiling water and cook for 12 to 14 minutes, or until water is absorbed.

2. Remove quinoa from heat and place in bowl. Add remaining ½ teaspoon sea salt, red pepper flakes, 3 tablespoons lemon juice and zest, brown rice syrup, mustard, and remaining 2 tablespoons olive oil.

3. Heat a small pot over medium-low heat. Add remaining 2 teaspoons olive oil, chickpeas, remaining 1 tablespoon lemon juice, red pepper flakes, and pinch sea salt. Cook about 4 minutes. Remove from heat and set aside.

4. To serve, scoop warm quinoa into serving bowls. Top with small piles of chickpeas, almonds, dill, and beets.

Pad Thai with Tamarind and Lime

GLUTEN-FREE

30 MINUTES OR LESS

Serves 4 to 6

Prep time: 10 minutes

Cook time: 12 minutes

FOR THE SAUCE

1½ tablespoons Sriracha

3 tablespoons evaporated
cane sugar

¼ cup brown rice syrup

⅓ cup tamari

3 tablespoons freshly squeezed
lime juice

1 tablespoon fresh ginger, finely grated

3 tablespoons tamarind paste

FOR THE NOODLES

1 (16-ounce) package brown rice
pad thai noodles

2 tablespoons refined coconut oil

2 shallots, finely chopped

2 baby bok choy,
cut into ¼-inch-thick strips

1 cup fresh bean sprouts

5 scallions, cut into 2-inch pieces

⅓ cup dry-roasted peanuts,
coarsely chopped

2 limes, cut into wedges

Some would argue that pad thai has overtaken spaghetti and meatballs as North America's favorite noodle dish. There's something about the combination of sweet, salty, tangy, and crunchy that keeps that Thai joint on the corner in your phone's favorites. Now there's no need to give them a ring because you have this easy recipe at your fingertips.

TO PREPARE THE SAUCE

In a mixing bowl, combine Sriracha, sugar, brown rice syrup, tamari, lime juice, ginger, and tamarind paste. Whisk until uniform and set aside.

TO PREPARE THE NOODLES

1. In a large pot, bring plenty of water to a boil and cook noodles according to package directions, stirring frequently with pasta spoon. Drain, rinse well with cold water, and set aside.

2. Heat wok or large sauté pan over medium-high heat and add oil. Add shallots and cook about 1 minute. Add bok choy. Cook 2 more minutes. Add noodles and sauce and cook 3 to 5 minutes. Stir in bean sprouts and scallions. Cook 1 to 2 more minutes and remove from heat.

3. To serve, sprinkle each portion with peanuts and garnish with lime wedges.

TIP Most foods, such as tomatoes, carrots, and beans, have dozens if not hundreds of varieties. With tamarind, however, there's only one variety of the tree, which we think is awesome.

Creamy Vodka Pasta with Spring Peas and Bacon

Serves 4 to 6
Prep time: 12 minutes
Cook time: 28 minutes

FOR THE PASTA

1 tablespoon sea salt

1 (16-ounce) package pasta shells

1½ cups frozen peas

1 tablespoon extra-virgin olive oil (optional)

FOR THE SAUCE

2 cups unsweetened almond milk

½ cup vodka

1 (14.5-ounce) can diced tomatoes, drained

2 tablespoons freshly squeezed lemon juice

2 tablespoons red wine vinegar

1 tablespoon brown rice syrup

1 cup raw cashews

2 cloves garlic, finely chopped

2 tablespoons nutritional yeast

½ teaspoon sea salt

¼ teaspoon freshly ground black pepper

1 tablespoon vegan butter

12 to 15 cremini mushrooms, diced

1 (6-ounce) package vegan bacon (about 9 strips)

Sometimes you just want a light bite. This dish is not for those occasions. For one thing, it's rich, filling, and loaded with cashew cream, which would be more than enough to call it a night. But we don't stop there—this recipe keeps the party going with a hearty pour of vodka. The shell-shaped pasta perfectly holds the peas, smoky bacon, and mushrooms that round out this crowd-pleaser.

TO PREPARE THE PASTA

Fill a 6-quart pot three-quarters full with water. Add sea salt and bring to a boil. Add pasta and cook according to package directions. During last minute of cooking, add peas and allow to boil together. Drain through a strainer and toss with oil (use oil only if sauce isn't ready).

TO PREPARE THE SAUCE

1. While pasta is cooking, in a high-powered blender or food processor, combine almond milk, vodka, tomatoes, lemon juice, vinegar, brown rice syrup, cashews, garlic, nutritional yeast, sea salt, and pepper. Blend until completely smooth. Set aside.

2. Heat a 4-quart saucepan over medium heat and add butter. Add mushrooms and bacon, and cook for 4 to 6 minutes. Reduce heat to medium-low and add sauce mixture to pan. Cook for 8 more minutes, or until sauce is thick and creamy, stirring constantly.

3. Combine pasta with sauce. Serve warm.

TIP For best results, the sauce for this dish must be very smooth, so be sure your blender or food processor is up to the task before you begin!

Saag Aloo (Creamy Indian Spinach and Potatoes)

GLUTEN-FREE

30 MINUTES OR LESS

Serves 4 to 6

Prep time: 10 minutes

Cook time: 15 minutes

½ cup soy milk creamer

⅓ cup raw unsalted cashews

2 large red or russet potatoes, peeled and cut into large dice (2½ cups)

3 tablespoons refined coconut oil

1 yellow onion, finely diced

4 cloves garlic, finely chopped

½ teaspoon garam masala

½ teaspoon ground turmeric

¼ teaspoon ground coriander

¼ teaspoon ground cumin, or whole seeds

½ teaspoon sea salt

2 tablespoons fresh ginger, finely grated, plus 1 teaspoon, divided

6 cups tightly packed fresh baby spinach

¼ cup freshly squeezed lemon juice

Some people are intimidated by the idea of cooking Indian food at home, but you'll be surprised at how easy it can be to make this authentic dish. Just be sure to get the right spices and your plate will be as pleasing as anything in Punjab.

1. In a high-powered blender, combine creamer and cashews. Blend until completely smooth. Set aside.

2. Bring a 4-quart pot of salted water to a boil. Parboil potatoes for 7 or 8 minutes. Drain and set aside.

3. Heat a large sauté pan over medium heat and add oil, onion, and garlic and cook about 3 minutes to soften. Add garam masala, turmeric, coriander, cumin, sea salt, and cooked potatoes. Continue cooking about 5 minutes, or until golden. Add 2 tablespoons ginger and cook 2 more minutes.

4. Add spinach in bunches, stirring occasionally to wilt. Add lemon juice. Continue to stir until spinach is completely wilted.

5. Add cashew cream and remaining 1 teaspoon ginger to pan and cook until potatoes have softened, about 3 minutes. Season with more sea salt, if desired. Serve warm.

TIP Spinach is a botanical relative of beet, chard, and quinoa and loves cool climates, if you're thinking of starting a garden.

Huaraches with Mushroom Chorizo Topping

GLUTEN-FREE

Makes 8 huaraches

Prep time: 20 minutes

Cook time: 12 minutes

FOR THE HUARACHES

2 cups masa harina

1 teaspoon sea salt

1½ cups warm water,
  plus more if necessary

1 tablespoon neutral-tasting oil

The Beach Boys reference huarache sandals in "Surfin' USA," and we like to think the song topped the charts because it made people hungry for this incredible Mexican dish—a thick masa tortilla (shaped like the sandal that gives it its name) topped with a piquant mushroom-nut topping that would fool any sausage lover.

TO PREPARE THE HUARACHES

In a large bowl, mix together masa harina, sea salt, water, and oil and knead well. Knead in more water, 1 tablespoonful at a time, if needed to make a moist, yet firm dough. It should not crack at the edges when pressed. Cover in plastic wrap and let it rest for 2 to 3 minutes.

TIP When a recipe like this calls for a small amount of unique spices like ancho and guajillo chile powder, it's a great time to visit your local bulk bins spice section. The bulk bin is a convenient way to try out new spices without committing to buying a huge quantity.

FOR THE CHORIZO

3 tablespoons plus 2 teaspoons neutral-tasting oil, divided

2 cloves garlic, finely chopped

8 to 10 cremini mushrooms, finely chopped

1 cup toasted walnut pieces

¼ teaspoon cumin seeds

1 large tomato, seeded and diced

½ teaspoon sea salt

¼ teaspoon dried ground ancho chiles

¼ teaspoon dried ground guajillo chiles

¼ teaspoon dried oregano

¼ teaspoon smoked paprika

2 tablespoons freshly squeezed lime juice

¼ cup vegan sour cream (optional)

TO PREPARE THE CHORIZO

1. Heat a medium sauté pan over medium heat and add 2 teaspoons oil. Add garlic, mushrooms, walnuts, and cumin seeds and cook about 3 minutes, or until fragrant and golden.

2. In a food processor or blender, combine cooked mushroom mixture, tomato, sea salt, ancho and guajillo chiles, oregano, paprika, and lime juice. Pulse until uniform and well ground. Set aside.

TO PREPARE THE HUARACHES

1. Place ¼ to ⅓ cup masa dough in hand. Flatten into an oval about ¼ inch thick and 4 inches long. Repeat with remaining dough.

2. Heat griddle or large skillet to medium-high heat and add remaining 3 tablespoons oil. Place huaraches in skillet and cook for 4 to 6 minutes on first side and flip over. Top each huarache with 2 to 3 tablespoons chorizo and cook for 4 to 6 more minutes, or until lightly browned. Remove from heat.

3. Top each huarache with sour cream (if using). Serve warm.

Recipe
p.178

Desserts

Desserts conjure up visions of celebrations, parties, and happy occasions. There is a time and a place for a fruit plate, but no one wants to stick a candle in one for their birthday. That's why we're giving you a wide variety of cakes, donuts, and cookies that you can proudly serve to any crowd—and you don't even have to tell them it's vegan.

Vegan desserts can be as pleasing in taste, texture, and appearance as any sweet treat out there. Don't be intimidated if some of the recipes call for specialty pans, like those in our donut or stout cake recipes. If you don't have one of these pans, don't let that stop you. Just make the recipes into cupcakes, or a large cake, and adjust the baking time accordingly.

Vanilla Bean Ice Cream

Go-To Recipe

GLUTEN-FREE · NUT-FREE

Makes 1 quart

Prep time: 8 minutes

Cook time: 6 minutes,
plus 1½ hours chilling time

2½ cups soy milk creamer

¼ cup brown rice syrup

½ cup evaporated cane sugar

3 tablespoons arrowroot powder,
dissolved in 3 tablespoons
soy milk creamer

1 vanilla bean, split lengthwise

⅛ teaspoon sea salt

¼ teaspoon vanilla extract

TIP Be sure to put your ice cream
maker's freezer bowl in your freezer at
least 24 hours before making ice cream.

TIP You'll find arrowroot powder in
most health food stores. You may see
a small jar in the spice section, but keep
looking for a big bag near the flours in
the baking aisle, because getting a larger
quantity will save you some dough and
you'll have a big supply ready to make
ice cream anytime.

Anyone can purchase a pint of ice cream, but a homemade batch will put the store-bought stuff to shame. When you make your own ice cream, you can tailor it to suit your tastes—if you love chocolate chips, throw in an extra handful; if you love candied ginger, chop some up and toss it in. Making your own allows you to really make it your own. The variations for this recipe are pretty significant departures from the vanilla, because we couldn't resist including these to-die-for scoops!

1. Heat a small saucepan over medium heat. Add creamer, brown rice syrup, and sugar. Heat until sugar is dissolved, about 5 minutes. Add arrowroot mixture and stir until thick.

2. Add seeds of vanilla bean pod by scraping small seeds out with side of a paring knife. Stir well to incorporate seeds into mixture. Remove from heat.

3. Add sea salt and vanilla to milk mixture. Whisk to combine.

4. Let mixture cool completely, about 30 minutes on the counter, then 30 minutes to 1 hour in the refrigerator.

5. Transfer mixture to ice cream maker and process according to directions, about 30 minutes or when desired consistency is reached.

Variations

Zesty Lemon Cheesecake Ice Cream

Makes 1 quart

FOR THE ICE CREAM BASE

2½ cups soy milk creamer

½ cup evaporated cane sugar

2 tablespoons maple syrup

1 tablespoon freshly squeezed lemon juice, plus zest of 1 lemon

3 tablespoons arrowroot powder, dissolved in 3 tablespoons soy milk creamer

⅛ teaspoon sea salt

1 teaspoon vanilla extract

FOR THE ADD-INS

1 (8-ounce) container vegan cream cheese

2 tablespoons evaporated cane sugar

2 tablespoons freshly squeezed lemon juice

1 cup crushed vegan oatmeal cookies or gingersnap cookies

TO PREPARE THE ICE CREAM BASE

1.   Heat a small saucepan over medium heat. Add creamer, sugar, maple syrup, and lemon juice and zest. Heat until sugar is dissolved, about 5 minutes. Add arrowroot mixture and stir until thick.

2.   Add sea salt and vanilla to milk mixture. Whisk to combine.

3.   Let mixture cool completely, about 30 minutes on the counter, then 30 minutes to 1 hour in the refrigerator.

TO PREPARE THE ADD-INS

In a bowl, whisk cream cheese with sugar and lemon juice. In a separate bowl, crush cookies and set aside.

Transfer ice cream mixture to ice cream maker and process according to directions, adding lemon-cream cheese mixture and crushed cookies to ice cream during final 2 minutes of agitating. Serve when desired consistency is reached.

Coconut Ice Cream with Candied Ginger

Makes 1 quart

FOR THE ICE CREAM BASE

1 cup soy milk creamer

1 (13.5-ounce) can full-fat coconut milk

½ cup evaporated cane sugar

2½ tablespoons arrowroot powder, dissolved in 3 tablespoons soy milk creamer

⅛ teaspoon sea salt

2 teaspoons vanilla extract

FOR THE ADD-INS

¼ cup candied ginger, coarsely chopped

TO PREPARE THE ICE CREAM BASE

1. Heat a small saucepan over medium heat. Add creamer, coconut milk, and sugar. Heat until sugar is dissolved, about 5 minutes. Add arrowroot mixture and stir until thick.

2. Add sea salt and vanilla to milk mixture. Whisk to combine.

3. Let mixture cool completely, about 30 minutes on the counter, then 30 minutes to 1 hour in the refrigerator.

FOR THE ADD-INS

Transfer mixture to ice cream maker and process according to directions, adding candied ginger to ice cream during final 2 minutes of agitating. Serve when desired consistency is reached.

Peppermint Crunch Ice Cream

Makes 1 quart

FOR THE ICE CREAM BASE

2½ cups soy milk creamer

¼ cups brown rice syrup

½ cup evaporated cane sugar

3 tablespoons arrowroot powder, dissolved in 3 tablespoons soy milk

⅛ teaspoon sea salt

Dash vanilla extract

FOR THE ADD-INS

¼ teaspoon peppermint extract

⅓ cup vegan dark chocolate chunks

¼ cup crushed peppermint candies

TO PREPARE THE ICE CREAM BASE

1. Heat a small saucepan over medium heat. Add creamer, brown rice syrup, and sugar. Heat until sugar is dissolved, about 5 minutes. Add arrowroot mixture and stir until thick.

2. Add sea salt, vanilla, and peppermint extract to milk mixture. Whisk to combine.

3. Let mixture cool completely, about 30 minutes on the counter, then 30 minutes to 1 hour in the refrigerator.

FOR THE ADD-INS

Transfer mixture to ice cream maker and process according to directions, adding chopped chocolate and crushed peppermint candies to ice cream during final 2 minutes of agitating. Serve when desired consistency is reached.

Baked Confetti Donuts

Makes 12 donuts
Prep time: 20 minutes
Cook time: 22 minutes

No one will forgetti, if you make them a donut of confetti. These baked donuts look and taste way naughtier than they actually are, having half as many calories as a cupcake. Now that's what we call a party.

Preheat oven to 350°F.

FOR THE DONUTS

¾ cup unbleached all-purpose flour
½ cup whole-wheat pastry flour
½ cup evaporated cane sugar
2 teaspoons ground flaxseed
1 teaspoon aluminum-free baking powder
¼ teaspoon sea salt
¾ cup unsweetened almond milk or soy milk
⅓ cup neutral-tasting oil
2 teaspoons vanilla extract
1 teaspoon apple cider vinegar
2 tablespoons naturally dyed sprinkles
Cooking spray

FOR THE VANILLA GLAZE

1 tablespoon vegan butter, at room temperature
1¼ cups powdered sugar
2 teaspoons unsweetened almond milk, plus more as needed
½ teaspoon vanilla extract
⅛ teaspoon sea salt
1 tablespoon naturally dyed sprinkles

TIP To help loosen your donuts, give them a little twist in the pan after they've cooled. For the smoothest transition to the cooling rack, place the rack on top of the donut pan and flip them over together. After a few taps on the bottom of the pan, the donuts should come out easily.

TO PREPARE THE DONUTS

1. In a large bowl, combine flours, sugar, flaxseed, baking powder, and sea salt, and whisk until uniform.

2. Add almond or soy milk, oil, vanilla, and vinegar to the dry ingredients. Whisk until uniform. Fold sprinkles into batter.

3. Grease donut pan generously with cooking spray and pour 2 tablespoons batter into each donut section. Using a spoon, smooth batter around each donut section to leave an even surface.

4. Bake for 22 minutes, or until toothpick comes out clean. Let donuts cool on a cooling rack over a rimmed baking sheet.

TO PREPARE THE GLAZE

In a small bowl, combine butter and powdered sugar. Whisk until lumpy. Add 2 teaspoons almond milk, vanilla, and sea salt. Whisk until smooth. If too firm, add additional milk in 1-teaspoon increments.

Drizzle a small amount of glaze over each donut. Immediately sprinkle with sprinkles, before glaze hardens. Set aside to cool.

TIP Not all sprinkles are created vegan. Look out for cochineal, which is actually a red dye additive made from crushed insects.

Cognac Baklava Rolls

Makes about 12
Prep time: 12 minutes
Cook time: 32 minutes

FOR THE FILLING

1 cup toasted walnut pieces

3 tablespoons evaporated cane sugar

½ teaspoon ground cinnamon

⅛ teaspoon ground cloves

Pinch sea salt

1 teaspoon cognac or brandy

1 teaspoon freshly squeezed
    orange juice, plus zest of ½ orange

FOR THE SYRUP

⅓ cup water

1 cinnamon stick

¼ cup evaporated cane sugar

2 tablespoons agave

2 tablespoons brown rice syrup

1 teaspoon freshly squeezed
    orange juice

Pinch sea salt

4 sheets phyllo dough, thawed
    according to package directions

⅓ to ½ cup vegan butter, melted

2 teaspoons ground walnuts

Powdered sugar, for garnish

TIP Cognac is a type of brandy distilled in copper pots and aged in oak barrels. If you purchase a bottle for this recipe, you can mix up a Sidecar or Brandy Alexander and enjoy a postprandial cocktail.

We took a traditional recipe for baklava, veganized it, and shaved two days off the prep. You're welcome. We love making treats, but we refuse to spend needless hours in the kitchen because, just like you, we're busy! These baklava rolls spiked with cognac give you all the enjoyment of baklava, in no time at all.

Preheat oven to 350°F.

TO PREPARE THE FILLING

In a food processor, combine all filling ingredients. Pulse until uniform.

TO PREPARE THE SYRUP

In a small pot, combine all syrup ingredients. Cook for 5 to 8 minutes, or until mixture thickens. Remove cinnamon stick and set aside to cool.

TO PREPARE THE ROLLS

1. Unfold sheets of phyllo. Place 1 sheet on a clean surface. Cover unused phyllo with a damp kitchen towel. Brush phyllo generously with some melted butter. Repeat with remaining 3 sheets, layering sheets on top of one another.

2. Place walnut mixture evenly on lower half of layered phyllo. Roll up from bottom in a tight roll. Slice diagonally into 2-inch pieces. Place pieces on a greased or silicone baking mat-lined baking sheet and generously brush with butter.

3. Bake for 25 minutes, or until golden brown.

4. Using tongs, dip hot rolls into cooled syrup. Cover and refrigerate in syrup, or serve immediately.

All-American Blueberry Buckle

NUT-FREE
Serves 6 to 8
Prep time: 15 minutes
Cook time: 48 minutes

FOR THE TOPPING

¼ cup packed brown cane sugar

2 tablespoons vegan butter

2 tablespoons unbleached all-purpose flour

2 tablespoons whole-wheat pastry flour

¼ teaspoon ground cinnamon

Pinch freshly grated nutmeg

Pinch sea salt

FOR THE BATTER

½ cup vegan butter

⅔ cup evaporated cane sugar

½ cup vegan sour cream

2 tablespoons maple syrup

1 teaspoon vanilla extract

1 cup whole-wheat pastry flour

½ cup unbleached all-purpose flour

2 teaspoons aluminum-free baking powder

½ teaspoon baking soda

¼ teaspoon sea salt

¼ teaspoon ground cinnamon

⅛ teaspoon ground allspice

2 teaspoons Ener-G Egg Replacer

½ teaspoon apple cider vinegar

¼ cup soy milk creamer

1 pint fresh blueberries, washed and patted dry

Powdered sugar for dusting (optional)

Blueberries add the perfect sweetness and tartness to this coffee cake cousin. And the streusel topping turns it into a classic buckle. We had to give you a taste of the old school, with a new school vegan twist.

Preheat oven to 350°F.

TO PREPARE THE TOPPING

In a large bowl, combine sugar, butter, flours, cinnamon, nutmeg, and sea salt. Incorporate with fork until crumbly and uniform. Set aside.

TO PREPARE THE BATTER

1. In a large mixing bowl or the bowl of a standing mixer, cream together butter and sugar. Add sour cream, maple syrup, and vanilla and whisk until uniform. Set aside.

2. In a large bowl, combine flours, baking powder, baking soda, sea salt, cinnamon, allspice, and egg replacer. Whisk.

3. Slowly add dry ingredients to creamed mixture, then add vinegar and creamer. Whisk until smooth. Fold in blueberries.

TO PREPARE THE BUCKLE

1. Spread batter into greased 9-inch springform pan. Sprinkle topping evenly over batter. Bake for 45 to 48 minutes, or until a toothpick comes out clean.

2. Cool on cooling rack and top with powdered sugar (if using).

TIP Blueberries are delicate little things. When buying them, make sure they have a plump, uniform look, in a container free from moisture. Keep them covered in the refrigerator and they'll last up to 3 days.

Individual Chocolate Stout Cakes

Makes 12 personal cakes
Prep time: 10 minutes
Cook time: 32 minutes

1 cup unbleached all-purpose flour

¾ cup whole-wheat pastry flour

¾ cup evaporated cane sugar

¼ cup unsweetened cocoa powder

1 teaspoon aluminum-free
baking powder

¼ teaspoon sea salt

¼ teaspoon ground allspice

¼ teaspoon ground cinnamon

2 teaspoons ground flaxseed

⅔ cup unsweetened almond milk

½ cup dark vegan beer

⅓ cup neutral-tasting oil

3 tablespoons maple syrup

1 teaspoon vanilla extract

3 tablespoons vegan dark
chocolate chips

1 tablespoon powdered sugar,
for topping

Dark beer + chocolate bring out the best in each other, sort of like coffee + the morning. Combining these two into a single baked goodie just feels right. The cake is moist and elegant, while the stout adds notes of toffee and caramel. Since you only use a little beer for the recipe, guess who gets to have a little drink with dessert?

1. Preheat oven to 350°F.

2. In a medium bowl, whisk flours, sugar, cocoa powder, baking powder, sea salt, allspice, cinnamon, and flaxseed.

3. Slowly whisk in almond milk, beer, oil, maple syrup, and vanilla into dry ingredients until mixture is uniform and smooth. Fold in chocolate chips.

4. Grease a 12-cake mini Bundt pan and pour batter into each section, filling each cup three-quarters full. Bake for 30 to 32 minutes or until toothpick comes out clean. Let cakes cool completely. Sift powdered sugar over the tops and serve.

TIP   Our favorite dark beers to use in this recipe are AleSmith Speedway Stout, or Sierra Nevada Stout. But any brand of dark vegan brewski will do.

Cappuccino Chocolate Bark

GLUTEN-FREE · NUT-FREE

Serves 4 to 6

Prep time: 3 minutes

Cook time: 5 minutes, plus
30 minutes freezing time

2 cups vegan dark chocolate chips

1 tablespoon finely ground espresso

½ teaspoon ground cinnamon

¼ teaspoon sea salt

10 to 15 vegan marshmallows,
roughly chopped

TIP This dessert is perfect for sharing, because you can place the large bark piece in the middle of the table, and guests can snap off the piece that calls their name. Everyone will be happy.

If real tree bark tasted as good as this chocolate bark, there'd be no forests left. Cappuccino flavors are conjured through finely ground espresso and marshmallows, enveloped in a chocolaty coating. There aren't many ingredients in this recipe, but each one adds something special.

1. Melt chocolate chips in a double boiler, or in a heatproof bowl over a small pan filled with 1 inch simmering water.

2. While chocolate chips are melting, add espresso, cinnamon, and sea salt. Continue to melt about 2 to 3 minutes, folding mixture occasionally. When chocolate is melted, fold in marshmallows to coat.

3. Line a baking sheet with wax paper and spread melted chocolate mixture as evenly as possible, about ¼-inch thick.

4. Cool on counter for about 10 minutes and transfer to freezer for 30 minutes to 1 hour, or until firm. Cut or break into uneven pieces with a knife and serve right away. Freeze whatever remains.

Cuban Coconut Rice Pudding

GLUTEN-FREE • NUT-FREE
30 MINUTES OR LESS
Serves 4
Prep time: 3 minutes
Cook time: 25 minutes

This recipe is our take on *arroz con leche*, a favorite in Cuba. Though the preparation is simple, the complex flavors of lemon, cinnamon, and sugar, combined with the smooth and creamy texture of the rice, keep you dipping in, bite after bite. Store this dessert in a tightly sealed container to enjoy it throughout the week.

FOR THE PUDDING

2 cups water

1 cup Arborio rice

½ vanilla bean, split lengthwise

2 cinnamon sticks

2 (1 inch-thick) slices lemon peel

¼ teaspoon ground cloves

1½ (13.5-ounce) cans full-fat coconut milk

½ cup evaporated cane sugar

Pinch sea salt

¼ cup raisins or currants

FOR THE TOPPING

2 teaspoons evaporated cane sugar

¼ teaspoon ground cinnamon

TO PREPARE THE PUDDING

1. In a large saucepan, bring water to a simmer, with lid on. Add rice and stir gently. Add vanilla bean, cinnamon sticks, lemon peel, and cloves. Simmer, partially covered, over low heat for 12 to 15 minutes, or until rice is tender and liquid is almost absorbed.

2. Stir in coconut milk, sugar, sea salt, and raisins or currants. Cook for an additional 8 to 10 minutes, stirring frequently.

TO PREPARE THE TOPPING

In a small bowl, stir together sugar and cinnamon.

Remove rice pudding from heat and spoon into small glasses or cups. Top with cinnamon sugar. Serve warm or chilled.

TIP White Arborio rice is the only rice you can use for this dessert. Brown rice simply won't work (as much as we all love it and wish it did).

Sticky Bourbon Pecan Pie Bars

GLUTEN-FREE

Makes 12 bars

Prep time: 12 minutes

Cook time: 16 minutes,
plus 1 hour 20 minutes to cool

FOR THE CRUST

¾ cup all-purpose gluten-free
  flour blend

¾ cup gluten-free rolled oats

3 tablespoons evaporated cane sugar

½ teaspoon aluminum-free
  baking powder

¼ teaspoon ground cinnamon

⅛ teaspoon sea salt

3 tablespoons neutral-tasting oil

2 tablespoons maple syrup

FOR THE TOPPING

2 tablespoons vegan butter

2 tablespoons all-purpose
  gluten-free flour

2 tablespoons bourbon

1 teaspoon vanilla extract

¼ cup maple syrup

¼ cup brown rice syrup

1 tablespoon molasses

¼ teaspoon ground cinnamon

⅛ teaspoon sea salt

1¼ cups toasted pecan pieces

These bars have all the flavor and sticky delicious-
ness of pecan pie, without the intensive work.
To top it off, they are gluten-free.

Preheat oven to 350°F.

TO PREPARE THE CRUST

1. In a food processor, combine flour, oats, sugar, baking
powder, cinnamon, sea salt, oil, and maple syrup. Pulse
until uniform.

2. Press mixture into greased 8-by-8-inch baking dish
and bake for 15 to 16 minutes, or until golden. Remove
from oven and set aside.

TO PREPARE THE TOPPING

1. While crust is baking, in a small saucepan over
medium heat, combine butter and flour. Whisk to form
a roux (a paste). Cook 1 minute, or until flour has a light
toasted color and fragrance. Be careful not to burn.

2. Add bourbon, vanilla, maple syrup, brown rice
syrup, molasses, cinnamon, and sea salt. Stir to combine
and continue to cook over medium-low heat for about
6 minutes, or until thickened. Add pecan pieces and
gently whisk. Cook about 1 more minute and remove
from heat.

3. Spread filling mixture over baked, slightly cooled
crust. Allow to firm up for 20 minutes on countertop
and then 1 hour in refrigerator.

TIP Pecan trees can live up to 300 years. They grow throughout
the United States, mostly in Texas, Oklahoma, Georgia, and
New Mexico.

Amaretto-Pecan Biscotti

Makes about 20 biscotti
Prep time: 12 minutes
Cook time: 50 minutes

6 tablespoons vegan butter

2 tablespoons vegan cream cheese

2 tablespoons vegan sour cream

¼ cup maple syrup

¾ cup evaporated cane sugar or
 maple crystals, divided

1 teaspoon vanilla extract

3 tablespoons amaretto liqueur

2 cups unbleached all-purpose flour,
 plus more for rolling and shaping

½ teaspoon sea salt

½ cup pecans, toasted and
 finely ground

TIP This dough can be a bit sticky,
so dampen your hands with water
to form the loaves.

It feels counterintuitive to make a dry cookie on purpose, but these crunchers are meant for dunking in coffee, *vino*, or a glass of almond milk. The beverage softens them up nicely but leaves a hint of crispness, creating the perfect bite.

1. Preheat oven to 350°F.

2. Using a mixer or a pastry whisk, cream butter, cream cheese, sour cream, maple syrup, and ½ cup cane sugar or maple crystals together until smooth. Add vanilla and amaretto. Whisk until uniform and creamy.

3. Add flour, sea salt, and pecans. Whisk just until a ball of dough forms. Do not overmix.

4. To make biscotti, dust countertop with flour. Divide dough in half and form into two ¾-inch-thick rectangular loaves. Grease a baking sheet and place loaves on sheet, about 2 inches apart. Sprinkle loaves with remaining ¼ cup cane sugar or maple crystals.

5. Bake for 25 to 30 minutes, or until rectangles look golden brown around edges.

6. Remove from oven and cut into long strips, 1 inch thick. Reduce oven heat to 300°F. Turn cookies onto a flat side and bake for 15 to 20 minutes, flipping cookies once. Alternatively, after turning cookies on their side, return them to oven and turn oven off, letting cookies crisp in oven overnight. The warmth of the oven will dry them out.

Pistachio-Cranberry Popcorn Balls

GLUTEN-FREE
30 MINUTES OR LESS

Makes 10 balls

Prep time: 12 minutes

Cook time: 4 minutes

¼ cup vegan butter

2 cups vegan marshmallows, roughly chopped

¼ teaspoon ground cinnamon

⅛ teaspoon sea salt

5 cups popped popcorn

1 teaspoon vanilla extract

⅓ cup shelled pistachios, coarsely chopped

⅓ cup dried cranberries, coarsely chopped

If you need a quick dessert for your friends or family over the holidays, make these balls! They're gluten-free, easy to whip up, and combine sweetness with crunch for a small, well-rounded treat!

1. In a 4- to 6-quart heavy saucepan, combine butter, marshmallows, cinnamon, and sea salt. Cook for 3 to 4 minutes. Turn off heat and add popcorn, vanilla, pistachios, and cranberries. Stir well, mixing until uniform.

2. Use a ½-cup measuring cup to portion out the mixture into 10 balls and place on a baking sheet lined with parchment or wax paper.

3. Let cool completely and enjoy.

TIP Did you know popcorn is a special type of corn? It has a hard outer hull and a starchy middle. When heated, pressure builds up in the interior of the kernel, and at its breaking point, it goes pop!

Gingerbread Cake with Buttery Rum Icing

Serves 10 to 12
Prep time: 15 minutes
Cook time: 44 minutes

Walking in a winter wonderland tastes a lot better with a slice of this cake in your cold little hands. With a kick from both ginger and cinnamon, it's guaranteed to warm you from your earmuffs to your snowshoes.

Preheat oven to 350°F.

FOR THE CAKE

1½ cups unbleached all-purpose flour
½ cup whole-wheat pastry flour
½ teaspoon ground cinnamon
¼ teaspoon ground allspice
¼ teaspoon ground cardamom
¼ teaspoon ground cloves
⅛ teaspoon freshly grated nutmeg
2 teaspoons aluminum-free baking powder
1 tablespoon ground flaxseed
¼ teaspoon sea salt
½ cup evaporated cane sugar
1 cup unsweetened almond milk
2 teaspoons vanilla extract
¼ cup molasses
2 tablespoons fresh ginger, finely grated
⅓ cup neutral-tasting oil
Cooking spray

FOR THE ICING

2 tablespoons vegan butter, at room temperature
2 cups powdered sugar
2 teaspoons dark rum
1 tablespoon plus 1 teaspoon soy milk creamer
⅛ teaspoon sea salt

TO PREPARE THE CAKE

1. In a medium bowl, whisk together flours, cinnamon, allspice, cardamom, cloves, nutmeg, baking powder, flaxseed, sea salt, and sugar. Add almond milk, vanilla, molasses, ginger, and oil. Whisk until smooth.

2. Grease a Bundt pan with cooking spray and pour batter into pan. Bake for 42 to 44 minutes or until toothpick comes out clean. Set aside on cooling rack to cool completely.

TO PREPARE THE ICING

In a mixing bowl, whisk together butter, powdered sugar, rum, creamer, and sea salt until smooth.

To glaze, place cake on a cooling rack over a baking sheet. Drizzle icing over entire cake, using baking sheet to collect excess icing, for ease of cleanup.

TIP The spices and ginger in this recipe actually help warm up your body, which is why people make this dish in the cold weather months. Ginger can help boost your immune system and fight infection—a bonus when everyone else is sick and you're eating cake to stay healthy.

German Chocolate Hand Pies

Makes 8 hand pies
Prep time: 15 minutes
Cook time: 26 minutes

We love holding hands, and to be perfectly honest, we love holding hand pies just as much. This pie is loaded with melty chocolate and crunchy nuts, all folded into a flaky envelope.

FOR THE CARAMEL

1 tablespoon vegan butter

1 teaspoon virgin coconut oil

2 tablespoons maple syrup

2 teaspoons evaporated cane sugar

¼ teaspoon sea salt

¼ teaspoon ground cinnamon

8 large Medjool dates,
  pitted and coarsely chopped

¼ cup unsweetened almond
  or soy milk

FOR THE PIES

½ cup shredded unsweetened
  coconut

1 cup toasted pecan halves
  and pieces

½ teaspoon almond extract

½ teaspoon vanilla extract

1 package vegan puff pastry,
  thawed (two 9-inch sheets)

¼ cup vegan chocolate chips

TIP Store leftover hand pies in foil. They will be good for up to 2 days. Reheat in a toaster oven to serve warm.

Preheat oven to 400°F.

TO PREPARE THE CARAMEL

In a high-powered blender or food processor, combine butter, oil, maple syrup, sugar, sea salt, cinnamon, dates, and almond or soy milk. Blend until smooth and creamy.

TO PREPARE THE PIES

1. In a large bowl, stir together coconut, pecans, almond extract, vanilla, and caramel sauce. Stir and set aside.

2. Slice each sheet of puff pastry into quarters. Add about 3 tablespoons pecan-caramel mixture to each square, off center, but leaving a ½-inch border around edge. Top pecan-caramel mixture with about 2 teaspoons chocolate chips.

3. Fold puff pastry to enclose filling, yielding a rectangle shape. Press all edges to seal, either with fingers crimping edge, or with a fork pressing a ¼-inch border around edges of each hand pie. Poke a few holes in top of each hand pie to allow air to escape.

4. Line a baking sheet with parchment paper. Place pies on sheet and bake for 24 to 26 minutes, or until browned and crisp.

Grilled Cinnamon Sugar-Cream Cheese Roll-Ups

NUT-FREE • **30 MINUTES OR LESS**

Serves 2 to 4

Prep time: 5 minutes

Cook time: 8 minutes

4 sheets whole-grain lavash bread

2 cups vegan cream cheese

1 teaspoon ground cinnamon

2 tablespoons evaporated cane sugar

¼ teaspoon sea salt

1 teaspoon neutral-tasting oil

We created this roll-up knowing that sometimes you don't have a lot of time, or a bunch of ingredients in the refrigerator, but still crave a sweet treat. They make a great snack or light dessert, and you can even call them a quickie churro.

1. Preheat oven to 350°F.

2. Place lavash bread on a flat surface and spread each sheet with ½ cup cream cheese.

3. In a small bowl, combine cinnamon, sugar, and sea salt, and whisk until uniform. Sprinkle each sheet lavash with an even sprinkling of cinnamon mixture, reserving some for the top of the roll-ups.

4. Roll lavash up lengthwise. Cut each roll across the center and then cut each half on a diagonal, yielding 4 pieces per roll.

5. Brush each roll-up with a little oil and sprinkle with remaining cinnamon sugar. Place on a baking sheet and bake 6 to 8 minutes, or until edges are slightly crisp. Serve warm.

TIP There are at least 2,000 species of cinnamon trees. They are related to avocado and bay trees.

Toasted Marshmallow–Pecan Milkshake

GLUTEN-FREE
30 MINUTES OR LESS
Makes 3 cups
Prep time: 5 minutes
Cook time: 1 minute

8 vegan marshmallows

1 pint Vanilla Bean Ice Cream (page 171) or purchased vegan vanilla ice cream

⅔ to 1 cup unsweetened almond milk

¼ cup toasted and salted pecan pieces, coarsely chopped

Smoothies schmoothies—sometimes you need a shake. This milkshake is not disguising itself as health food, so don't "eat one for breakfast, another for lunch, and eat a sensible dinner." We recommend serving in a large glass with two straws—one for you and one for your sweetheart—just like they used to in malt shops.

1. Poke 2 marshmallows onto end of a metal skewer, and scorch over an open flame. Once aflame, blow out immediately. Repeat with remaining marshmallows. Set aside on a wax paper-lined plate.

2. In a blender, combine ice cream and almond milk and blend until smooth, working quickly so ice cream doesn't melt. For a thicker shake, add more ice cream, or for a thinner consistency, add more almond milk. Add pecans and all but 2 toasted marshmallows. Blend for just a few seconds to incorporate.

3. Divide mixture among glasses. Cut reserved toasted marshmallows in half and place on top of each glass as garnish.

TIP Vegan marshmallows are now easy to find at your local health food store. In some parts of the country, you can even find them at Target!

Party On!

Sushi Night

Why are sushi hand rolls the perfect party food?

a) Everyone can put their choice of fillings inside.
b) You don't have to buy a bunch of sushi mats.
c) The meal pairs perfectly with hot sake.
d) All of the above.

➡ Baked Tofu–Avocado Hand Roll or Variations

➡ Sesame Miso Soup with Ginger and Tofu

➡ Asian Cucumber and Sea Vegetable Salad

Summer Beach Party

These dishes make eating on the beach a pleasure because they're easily transported, and don't fill you up, so you'll keep afloat and out of Davy Jones' locker.

➡ Tempeh Tuna Salad Wraps

➡ Bayou Coleslaw

➡ Baked Confetti Donuts

Date Night at Home

This special occasion deserves its own national holiday, and a classy menu. Make it memorable with a glass of full-bodied, grassy Sauvignon Blanc.

➡ French Pistou Soup

➡ White Bean Provençal Stuffed Zucchini

➡ Roasted Beet Caprese Salad with Toasted Walnuts

Mexican Fiesta

Whether you're celebrating a birthday, bachelorette party, or anniversary, make it a fiesta with the dishes below! This theme pairs well with margaritas or ice-cold Mexican beer.

➡ Baja Battered Avocado Tacos with Pickled Red Onions

➡ Tortilla Soup with Ancho Cream Topping

➡ Mexican Street Corn and Black Bean Salad over Greens

Get the Kids Involved

Learning how to cook at a young age creates less-picky eaters and is a special bonding time for the whole family. The kids will love cutting out the puff pastry for the pizzettes and forming the burger patties.

→ Fresh Tomato and Basil Pizzettes

→ Quick and Easy Red Bean Veggie Burgers

→ Vegan Cobb Salad with Zesty Vinaigrette

Good Morning, Sunshine

Wakey wakey, it's time to cook vegan eggs and bakey. This menu will add a little spring in your step for the rest of the day, and we recommend roasting the hash first, and then moving on to the quicker items if you woke up hungry.

→ Ultimate Breakfast Sandwich with Secret Sauce

→ Oven-Roasted Sweet Potato and Tempeh Bacon Hash

→ Fresh and Spicy Bloody Mary

Sporkie's Steak House

This theme is one of our favorite cooking classes to teach because you get to serve dishes that are seemingly so meat-heavy, and rich— so turn the lights down low and put on some Sinatra when serving this meal. Suits and ties required.

→ Seitan Chowder

→ Smoky Shiitake Bacon Wedge Salad

→ French Dip Sandwiches with Walnut Jus

Resources

Here are a few of our all-time faves that will make cooking and eating vegan meals easy-peasy.

FOOD COMPANIES/PRODUCTS

Below is a list of companies that make great-tasting products that we use on a regular basis both in our cooking classes and in this cookbook. They are available in most grocery stores, both natural and conventional.

AUSSIE BAKERY Non-hydrogenated unbleached puff pastry

DANDIES Vegan marshmallows, mini and large

EARTH BALANCE Vegan butter for all recipes from baked goods to savory dishes

ENER-G EGG REPLACER We love that this brand has a neutral taste and binds well in recipes

FOLLOW YOUR HEART Vegenaise, cheese, cream cheese, dressings, VeganEgg, and sour cream

FRONTIER ORGANIC SPICES High-quality, non-irradiated spices, including Ceylon and Vietnamese ground cinnamon

IMAGINE Vegan "no chicken" low-sodium vegetable broth

KITE HILL Artisanal cheeses and yogurt

LIGHTLIFE Organic soy tempeh that has great texture and flavor

LUNDBERG Organic brown rice syrup and rice

MISO MASTER High-quality miso paste

SETTON FARMS California-grown pistachios, cashews, and our favorite snack, Pistachio Chewy Bites

SO DELICIOUS DAIRY FREE Almond milk and sweet treats

SWEET & SARA Vegan marshmallows

WHOLESOME Dry sweeteners, agave, molasses that are fair trade, organic, and non-GMO

WILDWOOD Organic soymilk creamer and organic tofu made with US-grown soybeans

THE WIZARD'S Vegan Worcestershire sauce

BLOGS/WEBSITES

There are so many aspects to veganism including travel, fashion, beauty, food, and the environment. We have friends who will shed light on each of these facets of the lifestyle and have done their research so you don't have to.

BARNIVORE *barnivore.com*
Great resource for finding vegan booze, from beer to hard liquor.

DRIFTWOOD MAGAZINE *driftwoodmag.com*
Explores travel and culture from a vegan perspective.

ECO-VEGAN GAL *ecovegangal.com*
Whitney offers an eco-conscious view of veganism and abundant resources like her YouTube channel.

JOYFUL VEGAN *joyfulvegan.com*
We love Colleen's inspirational and articulate view of what it means to be vegan.

OLIVES FOR DINNER *olivesfordinner.com*
Beautiful food photos and wonderful recipes by husband and wife team, Jeff and Erin.

THUG KITCHEN *thugkitchen.com*
Cook and laugh all at once with our friends Michelle and Matt.

VEGAN YACK ATTACK *veganyackattack.com*
Delicious recipes and gorgeous photos from our friend Jackie.

VEGNEWS MAGAZINE *vegnews.com*
A vegan lifestyle magazine that we contribute to on the regular!

RESTAURANTS

Here are some of our favorite restaurants from around the world that have created memorable vegan meals we will never forget. We hope this list inspires you to travel and eat!

FINE DINING
Crossroads Kitchen, Los Angeles, CA

El Sapo Dorado, Monteverde, Costa Rica

Hangawi, New York City, NY

Mud Hen Tavern, Los Angeles, CA

Plum Bistro, Seattle, WA

Ravens Restaurant, Stanford Inn, Mendocino, CA

Shojin, Los Angeles, CA

Tenryuji Shigetsu Temple, Kyoto, Japan

Vedge, Philadelphia, PA

All restaurants at the Wynn and Encore Hotels, Las Vegas, NV

CASUAL DINING
Bouldin Creek Café, Austin, TX

ChocolaTree Organic Eatery, Sedona, AZ

Follow Your Heart Café and Market, Canoga Park, CA

Happy Family Restaurant, Monterey Park, CA

Homegrown Smoker Vegan BBQ, Portland, OR

Nagi Shokudo, Shibuya, Tokyo, Japan

Native Foods, multiple locations across the US

Ras Rody's Roadside Organic, Negril, Jamaica

Seabirds Kitchen, Orange County, California

The Veggie Grill, multiple locations across the US

Timeless Coffee, Oakland, CA

Vinh Loi Tofu, Chatsworth, CA

Vromage, Vegan Cheese Shop, Los Angeles, CA

VEGAN 101 DIPLOMA

Congratulations!

You've graduated with flying colors—and
fantastic flavors—from the school of Spork Foods.
We loved making this book for you, and we hope that
you love every meal you make with these recipes.

SPORK FOODS

Acknowledgments

We have received so much support and love throughout our 10 years of being in business. We want to give a special thanks to the following people who are dear to our hearts:

Joshua Bell, Jeremy Engel, Evander Bluejay Engel, Diana Goldberg, Eddie Goldberg, Jeanette Zimmerman, Wilma Engel, John Engel, Carolyn, Eddie and all of the Minneapolis Bells, Elizabeth Castoria and the hardworking staff at Callisto Media, Bob Goldberg, Jackie Horrick, Martin Kruger, Katie Franklin, Erin Keys and the whole Follow Your Heart family, Paul Storm, Nancy Ward, Kate Lewis, Aurelia d'Andrea, Patrick Gookin II, each and every one of our amazing cooking students, Michelle and Matt of Thug Kitchen, Kristin Bauer van Straten, Colleen Holland, Jennifer Chen and our friends at *VegNews* Magazine, Mia, Lee and the Cohen Family, Anna Abbatiello and the Setton Farms Family, Jeremy Miller, Josh Temple, Hayley Norman, Jackie Johnson, Caroline MacDonald, Ari Solomon and Mikko Alanne, Merlin Camozzi, Jenna Bleecker, Al and Dee from Vegan Food Share, Tim Moore, Kim Kessler, Jamie Shapiro, all of our hardworking friends at PETA and Mercy for Animals.

Conversion Charts

Volume Equivalents (Liquid)

US STANDARD	U.S. STANDARD (OUNCES)	METRIC (APPROXIMATE)
2 tablespoons	1 fl. oz.	30 mL
¼ cup	2 fl. oz.	60 mL
½ cup	4 fl. oz.	120 mL
1 cup	8 fl. oz.	240 mL
1½ cups	12 fl. oz.	355 mL
2 cups or 1 pint	16 fl. oz.	475 mL
4 cups or 1 quart	32 fl. oz.	1 L
1 gallon	128 fl. oz.	4 L

Oven Temperatures

FAHRENHEIT (F)	CELSIUS (C) (APPROXIMATE)
250°	120°
300°	150°
325°	165°
350°	180°
375°	190°
400°	200°
425°	220°
450°	230°

Volume Equivalents (Dry)

US STANDARD	METRIC (APPROXIMATE)
⅛ teaspoon	0.5 mL
¼ teaspoon	1 mL
½ teaspoon	2 mL
¾ teaspoon	4 mL
1 teaspoon	5 mL
1 tablespoon	15 mL
¼ cup	59 mL
⅓ cup	79 mL
½ cup	118 mL
⅔ cup	156 mL
¾ cup	177 mL
1 cup	235 mL
2 cups or 1 pint	475 mL
3 cups	700 mL
4 cups or 1 quart	1 L

Weight Equivalents

US STANDARD	METRIC (APPROXIMATE)
½ ounce	15 g
1 ounce	30 g
2 ounces	60 g
4 ounces	115 g
8 ounces	225 g
12 ounces	340 g
16 ounces or 1 pound	455 g

Dirty Dozen & Clean Fifteen

A nonprofit environmental watchdog organization called Environmental Working Group (EWG) looks at data supplied by the US Department of Agriculture (USDA) and the Food and Drug Administration (FDA) about pesticide residues. Each year it compiles a list of the best and worst pesticide loads found in commercial crops. The Dirty Dozen represents fruits and veggies that tend to have the highest pesticide load (meaning you should certainly buy them organic when you can), and The Clean Fifteen tend to have the lowest pesticide load (though, again, we recommend buying organic all the time). You can use these lists to decide which fruits and vegetables to buy organic to minimize your exposure to pesticides and which produce is considered safe enough to buy conventionally. This does not mean they are pesticide-free, though, so wash these fruits and vegetables thoroughly.

These lists change every year, so make sure you look up the most recent one before you fill your shopping cart. You'll find the most recent lists as well as a guide to pesticides in produce at EWG.org/FoodNews.

Dirty Dozen

Apples	Pears
Celery	Potatoes
Cherries	Spinach
Grapes	Strawberries
Nectarines	Sweet bell peppers
Peaches	Tomatoes

In addition to the Dirty Dozen, the EWG added one type of produce contaminated with highly toxic organo-phosphate insecticides:

Hot peppers

Clean Fifteen

Asparagus	Kiwi
Avocados	Mangos
Cabbage	Onions
Cantaloupe	Papayas
Cauliflower	Pineapples
Eggplant	Sweet corn
Grapefruit	Sweet peas (frozen)
Honeydew melon	

Index

Gluten-Free Recipe Index

About the Authors

Los Angeles–based Spork Foods is a gourmet vegan food company owned and operated by sisters Jenny Engel and Heather Bell. They offer live vegan organic cooking classes in Los Angeles at Spork Foods. They previously authored *Spork-Fed*, their first cookbook, with a foreword by fellow fans Emily and Zooey Deschanel. Heather and Jenny are Chef Ambassadors for two major corporations. They teach all over the country and the world, reaching over 10,000 people a year. Next time you're in LA, please join a live cooking class! Heather and Jenny create a four-course, vegan, organic meal around themes such as Chinese, Thai, Comfort Food, BBQ, Fancy Pants, Spanish Tapas, and so many more. You can join the Spork Foods mailing list to see an updated list of classes on their website. Reach out any time! Email us at jenny@sporkfoods.com and heather@sporkfoods.com.